Written more like a juicy tell-all novel. The Colors of My Wings captivated me from the beginning...Zanetta invites us into her riveting life story filled with promise, change, pain, and ultimately restoration. Not only does she honestly and openly tells her story with insight into the secrets & pains that led down this particular dark & sinful path, but she allows us to walk with her into the light that guided her out.

--Nikki Brooks Author of " Be Drama Free" & "Do Gay People go to Heaven"

God is definitely working miracles in Zanetta's life... I felt an empathetic pain in my heart that I haven't felt in a long time. This is how I know that Zanettas' writing is the stuff legends are made of.

--Vernon Lucas
-- Author of "Standing in the Shadows of Street Legends

The Colors of My Wings

All rights reserved. No part of this book may be reproduced or transmitted in any form or by any means, electronic or mechanical, including photocopying, recording or by any information storage and retrieval system without permission in writing from the Publisher.

All scripture quotations are taken from
King James Bible & New Living Translation ®. Copyright 2012 ©

[2009-2011]

Self-Published (The Collins Christian Company)

Library of Congress Cataloging-in-Publication Data

Printed in the United States of America.

ISBN Number: 978-1-62050-373-7

Memoire /Faith/Inspirational

Editing: LCEG The Content Experts Hyan Thiboutot

Pagination: Zanetta Collins

Cover Designed By: **www.charleswebcorner.com**

Page Inserts By: Intricate Graphix Designs

Bio Image: Misti Blu Day/ WWW.MISTIBLU.COM

The Colors of My Wings

Dedication

First and foremost, this book is dedicated to my wonderful son, whom the Lord blessed me with and gave me charge over during his time here on earth. Initially, as

a new parent, I can't say that I was doing all that was required of me. Now I do better because I know better. Moreover, with the Lord on my side, I'm going to do my best to provide the best life that I can for my son.

It's because of God's mercy and grace that we're blessed! So, to my beloved son, friend and hero I can say with the help of the most-high God I will equip and prepare you for success, against all odds, because no matter what you'll have, the Word and way of God to direct your path.

Ultimately, I'm pleased when you please God! Son: it is my prayer that you enter with full understanding that you can do all things through Christ who strengthens you! Always remember that mommy loves you and next to God you are the best thing that ever happened to me!

The Colors of My Wings

This book is also dedicated to my cousin the late Katernia Aaron! Trina: I watched your life and I never expected your death, but the Lord knows what's best! I know that your life didn't turn out the way you expected; I know you had a lot of suffering, but guess what, love, you don't have to *suffer anymore*! I've learned that in life we tend to take unexpected turns and we head down paths that no one expects. But again, the Lord knows best! As crazy as it seems cousin, your death gave me life. I can't say that I would have wanted it that way, but it did!

So cousin: thank you for the breath that God allowed you to breathe into me. From here on out, as long as I have breath in my body, I will continue doing my best to give your kids and grand kids a better example to live by. Trina, my cousin, I'm signing out. Love you always. Your little cousin *"Chick!"*

Lastly, I dedicate this book to the word "change". Without change, the new Zanetta would not exist.

With God's help, I was able to change. He helped me do so many things, like change my heart, my mind, my soul, and my thought process.

I thank God for change. It's time to take this thing

The Colors of My Wings

to the skies and fly on wings of the Most High.

So, here's to you, change, and to new beginnings!

Forward

While reading "The Colors of My Wings," I found myself thinking; who was this book written for? The book was vivid and sometimes even uncomfortable. But it was loaded with scripture. I realized the book addressed church bigotry, which imprisons the free.

John 8: 32: Lets us know that knowing the truth will give you the crown of liberty. Zanetta honestly bares her path to transformation. As her pastor, I have witnessed her pursuit of God's plan with the same fervor for truth. Her honesty about who she was and has become allows a pliable platform (good soil) for God to minister wholeness and healing to those who need it.

I believe this book exposes the strategic plan of the enemy to insert his plan and will in our brokenness and wounds, where there is no word to safeguard us. Religion won't do the job all by itself; it will require a relationship with our Lord and Savior Jesus Christ. This relationship can supersede and suffocate the plans of the enemy, no

The Colors of My Wings

matter how extreme it is. We sometimes respond to homosexuality as if it is not subject to the power of God.

We approach those who are bound in a manner that causes homosexuals to defend and protect the only identity they know. Truly the power of love, wisdom, holiness and being rooted in God's uncompromising word will make a difference. In fact it will allow the bound to lay down their shackles, for the loving purpose of our creator! I call this a divine exchange. "The Colors of My Wings," is a testament to the joyous freedom that we find in Christ.

I pray that as you read this book, out of the glorious riches of Christ, His Spirit may endow you with power through His Spirit in your inner being and that Christ may dwell in your heart through faith. Further I pray that you will be rooted and established in the love of Christ Jesus. Many saints are empowered when they are blessed enough to grasp just how wide, how long, high, and deep the love of Christ truly is. What manner of man is this, that he would lay down his life for you and for me, to call us friend.

Truly his love surpasses all knowledge and when

The Colors of My Wings

desired can fill you beyond measure because of the fullness of his indisputable power. In the name of Jesus to every one of you, much love, I pray you enjoy your read!

Pastor Shauna K. Jackson

The Colors of My Wings

Acknowledgements

Honestly I don't even know where to start. But I am so grateful to the people that the Lord saw fit to place in my life, old and new! There are so many people that I would like to thank but if I forget anyone, please know and understand; it's an error the mind not of the heart and it might be a little cheaper to leave a few names out (laughing out loud)!

First I would like to thank my mother and the rest of my family for who I am today. Mommy: despite our past struggles, I am grateful for the woman you have become. No matter what we have been through, the adversities have made both of us much stronger women. I trust and pray that as a result of both of our growing pains, you will understand my story. Oh and don't get it twisted; I see the growth. I love you mommy. Now it's time to move forward!

To my sister Surhonda. We may be on different paths, but I want to say thank you for that one sentence you said to me, the one that you thought I never

The Colors of My Wings

listened to:

"Zanetta, you need to go to church!"

And I thank you for suggesting I stay home and not leave again and run from my demons. It's the best thing that I could have ever done!

Next, I would like to thank my Pastor Shauna K. & Elder Larry Jackson and the entire Oil of Joy Family Church. Family: thank you for loving me to life! When I met you guys I expected judgment but you gave me love. This actually made all the difference in the world. Thank you.

Oh how I love Jesus for placing you guys in my life. Unfortunately, some people think that when we are thankful for certain people they think we are praising the individual and not the man above, but that's not the case for me. I feel that the Most High knew what I needed and he gave it to me! He placed in my life an intelligent and informative teacher. Pastor Shauna you gave me guidance, a firm hold, swag, (which means a fly dresser) and of course you loved me to life as well! So I am grateful for the pure ministry that is rich in love.

The Colors of My Wings

Pastor: you loved me to life and I thank you for being a part of my life, transition and growth. Paw-Paw I can never thank you enough for all the hugs, smiles, and encouragement you gave me when I needed it most. Thank you for giving my son an example of how a real man should be. What a great example to live by. When it comes to family and marriage, you live openly as you live privately. Love you always, Momma Bear and Paw-Paw!

To my two mentors, Joan Thompson and Altemese Davis: ever since I was a little girl, you believed in me even when I didn't believe in myself. When I had nowhere to turn, you opened your hearts and your homes to me. You will never ever know how much you mean to me. Words could never express the love I have for the two of you. Again, thank you for giving my heart and my head somewhere to rest.

To my girl Telma "Tee" Bias: my angel thanks you for the invite to Oil of Joy. Thank you for loving me to life. I see you as my prayer warrior. You have never looked down on me. You have always supported me and loved me unconditionally. Thank you for always being there, no matter what it looked liked! You are truly my ride-or-die chick! Thank you for seeing more in me than I saw in myself!

To Apostle Sheldon McCray Sr.: thank you for not shunning me. Thank you for the many conversations along with the guidance, prayers and support that you gave.

To Stephanie McCray: there is one thing I want to thank you for specifically, that prayer. And in that prayer, for some reason, the Lord decided to speak through you. But while you prayed, all I heard was *be still Zanetta, be still!* That sealed it for me. In my own expression, *"enough said"*. Love you. Oh, yeah, we've got work to do. Lets Get It!

To my girl Jeanette "J Doc" Dockery: an unforeseen friendship, I pray forever withstands the test of time! Thank you for all the love, support, guidance, and countless prayers that you have selflessly given on my behalf!

To Sonya Ward: I never would have thought a Facebook friendship would turned out to be more. That just goes to show that you never know who God is using

The Colors of My Wings

to be his instrument in an individual's purpose and their progress! But you know what? I thank God because he knows what we need and when we needed it. I thank you for all the countless hours of coaching, consulting and development that helped me tremendously. Thank you for always having an open door! So cheers to you; here's to new bonds; here's to extreme motivation, guidance, and support! You are awesome. Love you lots!

To my girl Oneal: thank you from the depths of my heart. When I met you I was in a very dark place but you were definitely a light in that dark place. You gave me support in more ways than one. No matter what anyone says, no matter what people think, you are another individual that loved me to life! Our associates are absolutely clueless concerning how much you have supported me. In fact, many of them even whispered rumors such as: Is that your chick?

To Girlena, words could never express how much I appreciate you and ALL that you have done, the countless days and nights that we spent working on this book; And all of the words of encouragement and prayers. Some

The Colors of My Wings

people are roots and some people are branches, thank you for being a root!

Again to my son De'Vyon Amir Malik "Mighty King" Collins: I thank you. I thank you for all of the hugs and kisses that you give and all love that you show. You take such good care of mommy. You even wipe my tears away, as much as I hate you catching me slipping. Thank you for believing in me, no matter what it looked like! You are the reason I refuse to die! Forever and always, I want you to know that I gave my best with the help and guidance of the Most High! Always remember that if you hold on to Him, you will never go wrong!

And most importantly, THANK YOU GOD! Thank you for holding on to me and not letting go. Lord, I thank you for letting me know that even when I thought no one was there, you were.

Thank you for returning me back to all the hopes and dreams I had as a child. Thank you from my soul. I feel so special knowing that I have a special place in your heart and that you saw fit for me to carry out your work, even though I don't quite know what the big picture fully

The Colors of My Wings

looks like. I thank you that you saw fit to entrust me as a soldier in your army!

I give myself away so you can use me!

The Colors of My Wings

Table of Contents

Dedication		4
Forward		7
Acknowledgement		10
Introduction		19
About		21
Chapter 1	Blood on My Wings	24
Chapter 2	Mommy Dearest	31
Chapter 3	She's Gotta Have Me	41
Chapter 4	Return on Investment	57
Chapter 5	Tangled	63
Chapter 6	Bait and Switch	69
Chapter 7	Test Run	82
Chapter 8	Be All You Can Be	93
Chapter 9	Wild Card	101
Chapter 10	Fire and Desire	118
Chapter 11	The Awakening	125
Chapter 12	Tired of being Tired	133
Chapter 13	In too Deep	141
Chapter 14	The Messengers	150
Chapter 15	Recovery	153
Chapter 16	Hungry	

The Colors of My Wings

Chapter 17	Challenge	163
Chapter 18	Liberated	166
Closing Remarks		169

The Colors of My Wings

Introduction

"My father created the heavens and the earth; he also created me from Adam's rib. But my ancestor bit of the forbidden fruit. Henceforth, a choice was made, a choice of a destructive path thus leading me to my death! In my eyes, I came to see things in a clouded image; An image that seemed as if I had become the walking dead. The way I saw it was that all of my dreams, visions, plans, were just like me, dead. Then God said, "Enough my daughter; arise from your grave; arise from those ashes and walk my child." and I did just that.

I began to walk. But before I moved forward I made a conscious decision to walk the narrow path and put down that forbidden fruit. He was telling me to break the cycle, to turn down the fruit that He had already told me not to eat of in the first place. Now that I have chosen to be obedient unto him, he has begun restoring all of the desires of my heart. He has also quenched my thirst for the women that at one point I desperately desired. He took the thirst away and that desire became no more.

I celebrate life in its pure form. Thank you Lord for saving a wretch like me.

The Colors of My Wings

About

Zanetta Lee Collins, was born to Valerie and Luther Collins Jr. in Fort Ord, California. At the age of three her parents, divorce forced her mother to relocate back to her hometown of Cocoa, Fl., where her mother met and married (common law) Rudolph Murray. Rudolph did his best to provide a stable home. However, the abuse that Zanetta suffered didn't stop. For many years, Zanetta suffered verbal and physical abuse and was molested by a family member when she was about 4 or 5 years of age. Her mother was addicted to drugs nearly all of Zanetta's childhood; from age seven to twenty-four years of age.

This left a significant void in Zanetta's life. She felt disconnected, alone, and always longed for her mother. Little did she know that this would become her driving force to do better. Zanetta was determined not to follow in her mother's footsteps. She decided to channel her anger, hurt, and frustration into sports. This was the gateway to a better education and an opportunity to open doors for her future. However, during this journey, she suffered from depression, anxiety and homosexuality.

When Zanetta graduated from High School, she obtained a basketball scholarship. This journey would not be easy; she bounced around four colleges trying to find her way. During the process, she gave birth to a beautiful son De'Vyon Collins. Due to sheer determination, after five years, she obtained her BA degree in Psychology from Edward Waters College in Jacksonville, Florida. Now with a degree in hand, it was still difficult to find stable employment to provide for her son. Shortly after this, she decided to enlist in the United States Army. This too would present a challenge as medical concerns forced her to be medically discharged. With great reluctance, she returned to Cocoa, FL.

Up to this point, life was difficult and utterly unbearable. There were times she felt like giving up and throwing in the towel. But as they say, winners don't quit. Zanetta Lee Collins didn't quit. Zanetta was determined to pursue her dreams of becoming something bigger than the hand that had been dealt.

After being back in Cocoa for several years the real

The Colors of My Wings

journey began when she accepted the "Lord" as her personal savior on August 18, 2009. This was undoubtedly the best decision she had ever made. It was not until this time she began the journey of discovering who she really was and who she really belonged to.

After giving her life to Christ she attended Cosmetology school and became a licensed cosmetologist. All this within two years of giving her life to Christ. She is currently enrolled at Full Sail University pursing her Master's Degree in Media Design, while establishing her new company ZLC, Inc.

This book is evidence of hard work, dedication and faith. It is entitled "The Colors of My Wings". So when it comes to this young lady, sit back and watch the work of Gods miracles unfold before your eyes.

God's Way...

The Colors of My Wings

1

Blood on My Wings

...I'm just thinking about how good Christ has been to me, how far he has brought me...he said daughter, as the naysayers speak death watch me pour life, life upon you my beloved child. Let them watch the performance of miracles, signs and wonders as I work in your life because my plans are to prosper you and give you hope. I will use you and all your struggles for the uplifting of My Kingdom.

Truly, it's amazing how the mind operates. Many would ponder how someone so young could remember such horrific things? I was between the ages of three and five when I spent a great deal of time with my grandmother. At the time, my grandmother lived in a duplex. Living

The Colors of My Wings

with her were my Auntie and Uncle. Another uncle lived on the other side of my grandmother. I remember as kids, we used to climb in and out of the window between our houses. My grandmother's duplex had two bedrooms, my grandmother's room and Aunt Tracy and Uncle Steve.

That house was much like a playground to me, especially Aunt Tracey and Uncle Steve's room. I felt safe and I had tons of fun. I had fun playing in that house up until a traumatic life-changing event. I will never forget the day the dynamics changed. The walls had closed in on me to seemingly swallow me alive.

A peaceful innocent nap quickly turned into a nightmare. One day while sleeping in my aunts rooms I was awakened by the hands of a family member touching me.

He was touching me in all the wrong places and in all the wrong ways. Touching me in places that words can never begin to express, deep places where band-aids just won't go. These places were places that only God knows best how to repair, erase, heal and restore. He was touching me and I had nowhere to run, nowhere to hide and no one to call.

The Colors of My Wings

I was scared; really scared. My eyes filled with tears. They felt so full as I lay there, confused, afraid, and trembling as he held his hand over my mouth telling me to open my legs as he pried them apart. He couldn't care less about my fear or my innocence. I heard my heart beating so hard that I could hear it in my head, between my ears. As he took his private part out and rubbed it over my vagina, I felt afraid, disgusted, and sick to my stomach because he was not suppose to be touching my "pocket book."

Back then we called our vagina's "pocketbooks." And as young girls we were taught how to clean our "pocketbooks" correctly and never to let any one touch us there. As he got more aroused, his actions intensified. His eyes were opening and closing as he kissed me like I should or could or would even want to respond at such a tender age. He was breathing heavily and making all kinds of moaning sounds. I remember feeling sick, very sick. While he went through all the motions, I grew more frightened. I thought I was going to die. In a way, at that moment I did die inside.

I was confused. I didn't understand what was going on.

The Colors of My Wings

All I knew was that I did not like it. Then he tried to penetrate me. He actually strained and trembled and pushed and pulled at me to try to get his penis into my pocketbook. But it wouldn't go, thanks be to Jesus. I guess because I was so young it was not physically possible. So he continued to rub his penis all over me. As he groaned and moaned, he began to jerk his body. Then suddenly, he ejaculated all over me. As a young girl I couldn't explain this white stuff squirting over me. Yeah, nasty, sticky, dirty white stuff. He put it all over my stomach. I felt so sick. I was so scared, the entire time.

> *"In that moment I wished that someone would come home soon."*

All I knew was that I needed to be rescued. So I closed my eyes and wished someone would save me from this man. I needed someone, anyone, to come and get this man away from me. In retrospect, that desperate wish was my silent prayer.

The Colors of My Wings

After I prayed that silent prayer I looked out the window and saw my grandmother's car, which for me was a prayer answered. God ALWAYS hears our prayers, and although he might not answer when we want him to, he does answer and when he does; it is always on time. I remember once I saw her car I said, that's my grandmother. In that moment he firmly told me that if I ever told anybody what he had done, he would kill me. I got up from the bed and ran to the bathroom. I was so afraid. I got in the tub. I cried and scrubbed so hard I nearly scrubbed my skin off. I felt dirty. When I got out, I had to sleep in that same room. Once I fell asleep, it felt like I had slept for days. I didn't want to open my eyes but I thought that if I opened them, just maybe, the nightmare would end. But the fact still remained that whether my eyes were open or closed, I was already living a nightmare.

For many years, I tried suppressing my hatred, anger, and disgust but I couldn't. And because I couldn't, it began to consume me and manifest itself in other ways. I call those other ways… snares. Always remember the devil is slick and the devil always has tricks up his sleeves:

> *Then know for certain that the Lord your God will no longer drive them out of your land. Instead, they will be a snare and a trap for you; a whip for your backs and thorny brambles in your eyes, and you will vanish from this good land the Lord your God has given you.*
>
> *Joshua 23:13*

To me this scripture meant that he would no longer fight our battles in the natural; you must be able to identify the traps and battle ahead. Although you will struggle, ask and seek God for help, understanding all the while that if you don't, the person that God intended you to be will vanish. You can't allow life to cause you to miss out because you will never get to reap your harvest and you will miss your season. We as a people question God and say, why did you do this to me or, why did you allow this to happen? One of the things we fail to understand is that God is love. God doesn't make such despicable acts happen to his people, he is not the author of confusion. But if he allows it to happen, then clearly he knows that you are an overcomer and that means he knows that ultimately you will come out victorious because you are anointed to be an overcomer. Now, if your question is why, it's because he created you to get the glory out of your life.

To me, life is truly like a game of chess; yes we are pawns; yes the Lord and the devil are both playing this crafty mind game otherwise known as the battlefield in your mind, but end your latter will be greater. If you take the time to read the book of Job, his story tells you that Job lost his money, his livelihood, his cattle, his family, and his health. Even his wife turned on him and told him that he should curse God, but he didn't. He kept the faith, no matter what it looked liked in the midst of his storm. He kept the faith. We as people need to grasp that same concept: no matter what it looks like, God is in control. So if you can accept this as truth, from this point forward walk by faith and not by sight.

The Colors of My Wings

2

Mommy Dearest

I was about six or seven years old when I realized that my mother had a serious problem. Well, actually, more than one problem; she had several areas of concern.

...Anger

One of her problems was anger. I never really understood why she had tantrums and destroy everything and anything in her path. The older I got, the more it became evident to me exactly what the problem was.

...Exposed

My mother had many struggles. But her biggest struggle was addiction. She was a druggie. To be frank, she was a "Crack Addict."

...Reality can be a beast

Man oh man can you picture and your step dad was no more or less than, a "step" dad in every form of expression. When I say that I simply mean this pertaining to the type of man he was, is, and know him to be. He was the kind of man that would only give you what you needed. My stepfather would make sure you had the bare essentials and that's that. He's was not the type of man that would say things like…

"Hey baby girl, I'm proud of you" or

"Hey, you know I love you."

That simply was not his thing. For me as a child, I never understood that. I never understood the distance or the lack of warmth and affection or the coldness that reigned in my home. In my eyes, it was like hell in my house most of the time. My mother would come home high or zooted out of her mind more often than not. Some days she would not come home at all, and she would pull this act for weeks on end. I remember trying to hide the situation from my baby sister because I didn't want her dealing with the misery that was going on around us. I wanted to protect her and to spare her the pain that I felt. I wouldn't allow her to see me cry or get upset. I would even make up stories to cover my mother's non-sense, activities and excursions away from home, away from us. It was a burden that words will never explain.

The Colors of My Wings

I can even remember one of my cousins telling me that my mother was giving a dude some head for a small piece of "crack rock". Now how true was it, I don't really know. But can you imagine hearing that at such a young age? In retrospect, I can't believe my cousin dropped that on me like that. Who wants to know their mother trades sexual favors to get high? Not me. I didn't want to hear that. It was way too much information for me to process. You may never recover from hearing such horrific events about your mother. You just never get over them. For years we watched as my mother went from our home to rehabilitation programs and then back to the streets. This process recycled over and over again for years on end. At times when my mother was around I noticed that when she napped, she often woke up choking on her own blood because she had snorted so much cocaine. She had destroyed the septum in her nose. She ended up having surgery just to be able to sleep.

To date, I still have vivid memories of seeing my mother suffer from the afflictions of her addiction. I feared for my mother's life and dealt with her habits for over twenty-three years.

The Colors of My Wings

My mothers was in and out of our lives for most of my youth elementary school, high school, and some of my college years. As I grew and started coming into my own, I knew I had to get out. I got out by playing basketball. That was my ticket. I played ball and got out of dodge. I was so confused at times I even tried to kill myself, not once, not twice, but three times. I tried to hang myself and the rope broke. I tried to cut my wrist but the glass wouldn't cut. I even had a bottle of pills in my hands. All of a sudden I had a knock at my bathroom door just in time to distract me. I know now that I had the favor of God then. This saving grace was nothing but God. It was not my time or his will, because my father had bigger plans and a greater purpose for my life and I'm learning that now.

> *But I have spared you for a purpose, to show you power and to spread my fame throughout the earth.*
>
> *Exodus 9:16*

The Colors of My Wings

There are so many things that happened to me in my childhood; my mother was a crack addict, my drinking sprees; I was drinking beer out of a bottle at 2yrs old. As I grew I became more and more angry.

I can recall when my mom destroyed my favorite rocking chair. I was just a kid. The first time she had a fit I didn't know if it was because she wanted crack or just angry with my dad. She took my chair and threw it into the wall. I waited for all the pieces to land so that I could pick them up. I did exactly that, I picked them up and I took them away and fixed it, I even fixed the little music box. But the second time, she just completely destroyed it. As simple as that seems that still hurt me till this day.

My mother even tied me to a door and beat me over a pack of cigarettes.

As I got older I told myself that I was going to win in life because they were so many things that I could do well. For example; drawing, painting, singing, dancing, and just dreaming. Dreams like owning my own business.

The Colors of My Wings

Hope deferred makes the heart sick, but a dream fulfilled is the tree of life.

Proverbs 13:12

We as a people need to realize and understand that even if we feel as though we have been dealt this terrible hand of life or all the dreams that we have had in our past are lost, it's not true.

Hope deferred...key word "deferred"

This means that if you surrender your hope, you will post pone inner joy. Hopelessness makes us sick, but just because its deferred doesn't mean that all is lost. This is why it is so important to be prepared for whatever. In life you must always be ready. You have to be in position to receive the blessings that the Lord has stored up just for you. He never stops blessing us, he just has to keep some in storage for some of us. Your blessing may be on hold for your greater good. For some of us if our blessings are given to us too soon the value just might depreciate ahead of season. So God being the all-knowing God that he is rearranges things accordingly. He weighs the outcome of the value depreciating verses it maturing? He put it up like a stock or bond and allows the value of that dream, idea, and us for that matter, to mature. The bottom line is sometimes there are just some things that we are not ready for. Honestly if he gave it to us it might literally destroy us.

So again the only thing I knew that was going to get me out of Brevard County was my athletic skills and my game of choice was basketball.

That was my ticket, my ticket out of what I considered my hellhole. That's the way I saw it then. I took a sport and leveraged my exodus. I played basketball to get out, four years of "college basketball." But what started
out, as one of my loves and talents quickly became an issue for me, not because I didn't have love for the game, but it became very evident that my small statue would become a major challenge. My freshman year I got hurt not once but twice, my junior year I got hurt again and I had to have two knee surgeries. So it became

evident that "Zanetta" would not be headed to the WNBA.

The Colors of My Wings

3

She's Gotta Have Me

They say a lot of female ballers, dibbed and dabbed in same sex relations and during my college years; I had my first encounter with a woman. And if you don't know what I mean I will break it down for you; It seemed that all my life people always expected "Zanetta" to be gay. I was suspected of being a lesbian. But the thing of it, is even though I always felt different from every other female, I never considered myself a homosexual. As far as my facts I always had a boyfriend. Now I wasn't sleeping with anyone, but I always had a boyfriend. Even though I didn't lose my virginity until I was almost nineteen years old I still was attracted to men. But there was always something a little different about me; what I realize now that I didn't realize then, is maybe that difference is the "greatness" that my creator had instilled in me. Thank you for making me so wonderfully complex.

> *Your workmanship is marvelous-how well I know it.*
>
> *Psalms 139:14*

But part of that complexity was riding on that game of chess the devil on one shoulder and God on the other shoulder trying to recruit me. When we see things that are appealing to us, we think… ok that's it, and we think that it's ok to be where we are. So long as we are comfortable even if that's not the place God wants you, we just get caught up in flesh. Because it's comfortable we settle, and don't fight to say no. Too often we settle into that comfortable place. We want our lives to be filled with blessings that make us happy, but what have we sacrificed as Christ did to gain that happiness? Just a thought. We think its okay to just "do us" but no, it doesn't work like that. We are not here for us, we are here for the uplifting and edification of the Kingdom of

The Colors of My Wings

Christ. We should at least be a fisher of men; that's the minimum that is required of us, to live a Holy life and become fishers of men. But nevertheless, in my junior year of college, I found out just what this *snare was*...

"Is it"
Is it me or is it she...
Is it he or is it we...
Is it us...damn, I'm about to cuss...

It was Sept 17, 1997 about eleven in the evening. It was my twenty first birthday. My teammates and friends had snuck me a glass of champagne into my dorm room because I had not done anything to celebrate my birthday. That night, I had my first kiss with a woman.

Her name was Michele Ross. Michele and I had become friends the summer before my junior year in college. She was a very loving, kindhearted person, but for some reason there was more of it, but I couldn't put my finger on it. And one day she called me crying. I said, "What's wrong?"

Then she said, "My best friend doesn't love me

anymore."

And I was oblivious to what type of friend she was referring to. Her best friend was also her lover. Now, like I said before, I didn't know that at first but she finally confessed it And I said, "Ok if that's your "thang" then that's your thing." I wasn't mad. It just wasn't my cup of tea, at that time.

So as time went on we grew closer. She one day asked me if I had ever been with a woman. I said "hell no." Then she told me that she was attracted to me and didn't want to lose her girlfriend or my friendship. I had no intention on being with a woman. But our conversation grew more and more lengthy overtime.

She lived in a completely different time zone. We had a three-hour difference, but we would talk from seven o'clock to eight in the morning, then I would go to class from eight am to twelve noon, and even when I got out of class from twelve noon to two pm, we talked. I worked from two pm to eleven pm, on my lunch breaks and my fifteen-minute breaks we would talk, and when I got off at eleven pm we would talk until we fell asleep on the phone together. How crazy was that?

The Colors of My Wings

It got to a point, where I had become consumed with her, so I said to her one day, "I think I'm attracted to you too." She asked me to repeat myself but I was too scared to utter those words again. So we kept communicating and then one day she said to me, "Zanetta I want to do something for you," and I said, "Okay, what's up?" Now I'm thinking she had something to tell me or maybe she had written something she wanted me to hear. But no.

It got really quiet and she began masturbating on the phone and I was stunned. I was stunned and shocked, but it turned me on at the same time. It also scared me. I mean it really, really scared me. To know this female, same sex as me, same body parts as me, was masturbating over the phone. She turned me all the way on and it took me by storm, shock and surprise. It got so crazy I just threw the phone. I threw the phone fast and furiously. My sister came in the room and asked me, "What's wrong, Zanetta?"

I told my sister that nothing was wrong because honestly I was in a state of utter shock. My heart raced so hard I could feel the muffled pulse in my ears, and I felt like the room was shrinking and closing in on me. I sat there nearly paralyzed with fear and confusion.

Snare

There was a reason for my state of mind and the reason that it scared me so much, I actually liked it. I wasn't sure but it felt like I did and I could not figure things out. Now tell me how do you process that; how you deal with something so foreign to you? I sat there for hours. I didn't eat that night. I didn't move to go to the bathroom. I just stayed still with my mind recycling what had just happened. That vision was on loop in this head of mine.

Now, it was time for school to start up. So by the time the new school year rolled around we were both so discombobulated we didn't know what to do or how things were going to play out between us, because once again she had a woman despite what was going on between us and she had no intentions on letting her lover go, and I didn't want her to. She eventually told her girl that she had feelings for me and I kept fighting my feelings. But of course, as time grew, what I wanted - what I craved - didn't seem to subside. Instead, it intensified. The absence of it actually made my body ache for a true experience. I needed to take it there.

I eventually told her that I wanted a kiss, which brings me back to the night of my twenty-first birthday, Sept 17,1997 after everyone left my room. I will never forget how it got so quiet just before Michele came back to my room. She asked me what else did I want for my birthday. I told her I wanted that kiss. She sat on my bed; I leaned over and kissed her, but she pushed me away. I went and sat on the other bed. I was so nervous about the whole thing.

"Zanetta, what are you thinking? What the heck are you doing?" those thoughts ran through my head.

She asked, "Well did you like it?"

I replied, "I don't know, you pushed me away too fast." Then she was like, okay, come on. I got up off the bed and moved closer to her. Our lips touched. And at that moment I felt like time stood still. So much passion had been building up. She grabbed my shirt and pulled me

The Colors of My Wings

on top of her. And then, we just stopped. She pushed me away. I went and sat on the other bed and I started talking to myself, "Zanetta you just kissed a chick, a female, a lady... then I thought: Negro, she got the same thing you got."

But the fact remained: I liked it. I liked it a lot!
As a matter of fact it was the best kiss I had ever had in my little twenty-one years of life. After that kiss I wanted more, but I resisted for a while. Until one night.

She came in my room and fell asleep in my other bed. I was asleep and she was on the phone with her girlfriend when all of a sudden I hear moaning and panting going on. I woke up, but I didn't move. Instead, I just laid there. She was masturbating on the phone with her girl, but she knew I wasn't asleep and by this time she had told her girl what transpired between us and she told her that there was an interest for more.

So she says to me, "Zanetta are you asleep?" I said no. " I'm thinking: how can I sleep with all that going on next to me? She tells her girl that she would like to take things to the next level with me. She wanted to take it to that physical level by making out with me. It

The Colors of My Wings

couldn't be anything more than physical because she had her girl despite what had taken place or was about to take place between us. There were feelings involved, I suppose so much that she told her girl what she wanted point blank.

To be totally honest, I was shocked that her "girlfriend" told her to get on with me. If it was what she wanted, then fine. She didn't want to keep her from what made her happy. The only thing she wanted to do was to be on the phone while it took place.

I could not believe this crap. I was like, you guys are crazy. But my dumb self eventually gave in; because I wanted it so bad. So there I was and there she was sitting on my bed. I looked at her and she looked at me. Then we kissed. I kissed her on her hip. It then seemed as if she went crazy and I was like, dang, I did that.

Then I went a little further. Then a little further. And before you knew it I'd had my first experience with a woman.

Mind you, this all went down while her girlfriend was on the phone, which was total perversion.

The Colors of My Wings

...If a man practices homosexuality, having sex with another man as with a woman, both men have committed a detestable act. They must both be put to death, for they are guilty of a capital offense.

Leviticus 20:13.

Don't you realize that these who do wrong will not inherit the Kingdom of God? Don't fool yourselves. Those who indulge in sexual sin or who worship idols or commit adultery or are male prostitutes, or practice homosexuality.

1 Corinthians 6:9

In order to justify there sin, people will say the bible has been rewritten over and over again. This is true but, the fact still remains the "Word" in any translation is right. I even went back to the King James Version which states: know ye not that the unrighteous shall not inherit the

The Colors of My Wings

kingdom of God. Be not deceived; neither fornicators, nor idolaters, nor adulterer, nor effeminate, nor abusers of themselves with mankind. After reading that I said ok I don't see anything about homosexuality. But then I said to myself: Zanetta…what does effeminate mean?

I had never heard or read that word before. The definition of *"effeminate"* means of man having traits, considered feminine which means homosexual.

Some dictionaries will advise that it is having unsuitable feminine qualities. In other words; men having female qualities and females having male qualities. Either way, it is unsuitable, therefore, inexcusably unacceptable.

After my experience with Michele, I went and sat on the floor in my closet and she went and sat on the floor by the door. I got up and looked at myself in the mirror and just stared and stared while she sat crying on the phone to her girlfriend because she felt guilty. As for me, I was in utter shock about what had just happened. I looked in the mirror and asking myself, "Zanetta what the hell did you just do?" After that I ran to the bathroom and scrubbed my mouth like never before. I literally felt sick to my stomach. There was this strange ache in the pit of my stomach.

After my first experience, things got really difficult for me at school. It was particularly hard because Michele had her girl whom she would not leave for anyone. And what about me? Well let's just say I was just stuck with my heart in cuffs caring about someone that I would never ever have. Even though we knew there was something between us, we could never go down that path again.

As time went on, after our basketball practices, she would come to my room and I would give her massages, while trying to keep my feeling in check about my desire to be with her. Then afterwards she would jump up and leave. I would cry; because I could never have her. I felt like I had no control over what was going on inside me. I was literally feeling sicker and sicker over her.

One time I came home and a friend of mine asked me what was going on. I didn't respond at first. She said to me, "Zanetta, you have lost a lot of weight and I can tell something is wrong."

The Colors of My Wings

Eventually, I broke down and told her what I had been dealing with. She said, "Zanetta, you owe it to yourself to live your life and make yourself happy. Discern the

Snare

After that I sat out to do just that, live my life and make me, "Zanetta" happy. Not realizing at that age that I should've been being obedient and submissive unto God. Not that she meant any harm but I now know that my life is not about me, it's about Jesus. It's about submitting to his will, not my own will.

> *Submission, submit to God's royal son, or he will become angry, and you will be destroyed in the midst of all your activities, for his anger flare up in an instant. But what joy for all who takes refuge in him.*
>
> *Psalms 2:12*

The Colors of My Wings

We as a nation, as a people that are in this world, don't seem to understand that we are not of this world; we just live here.

> *In the beginning God created the heavens and the earth.*
>
> *Genesis 1:1*

Alien, Moses first son was named Gershom, for Moses had said when the boy was born, ' I have been a foreigner in a foreign land.

Exodus 18:3

Our Father created us in his image and because RI all the sin that we put ourselves in which, by the way, was not meant for us, causes us to not realize we have a choice and we begin to die. We become the walking dead when we choose sin over submission and obedience of our Father. Our dreams die, our visions die; in fact, everything that He has set forth before us begins to slowly suffocate and die.

> *Death, there is a path before each person that seems right, but it ends in death.*
>
> *Proverbs 14:12*

What we don't understand is; even if our dreams are dead, they can still come back to life. Who better to resurrect your dreams other than God, He who gave us life, He who created us? Who better than our Father whom art in heaven, to give us everything back? Surely not the devil because his goal is to steal, kill, and destroy.

The Colors of My Wings

4

Return on Investment

After my first encounter with a woman, I remember this female that had been trying to talk to me for the longest time. It was brought to my attention that she had an interest. I shut it down because I had no interest in women at the time. So I thought. But after my experience with Michele, who was someone that I could never completely have, why not try to be with someone that I could have or be with? So I did. We began dating. It was a long distance relationship. Now for me, it never mattered to me whether my relationship was long distance or not, as long as I knew I had someone to come home to. She didn't feel the same way. She wasn't fit for a monogamous relationship. She felt as though she could have her cake and eat it too. She did just that; until I caught on to what had been transpiring.

The Colors of My Wings

After finding out that she had been cheating on me, I came home because it was time for us to decide the fate of our relationship. Things did not go exactly as I expected them to. Instead of a civil and responsible conversation, we wound up arguing. Then she abruptly left me, alone, trying to figure out what had just happened. I later learned that and three other females had sex with another chick. Now get this; it wasn't even the chick I had already found out about. After that, this crazy female came back home where I was and we made love like nothing had ever happened. Who does this?

Now please keep in mind that I had no knowledge of any of her excursions when she came home. In fact, I found out later, at a point when I was in too deep, way too deep.

Eventually her games got so out of hand that she played herself right on out. We broke up despite the stronghold she had on me. She was a low down, trifling chick that had no regards for anyone beside herself. She couldn't care less about contracting anything or the next person's well being.

A few weeks after, we split up. My body felt

The Colors of My Wings

different, uncomfortable, and irritable. Something told me there was a problem and that I needed to check myself out. I did. I found a bump on my vagina. I grabbed my aunts' medical book. Herpes! My eyes were as huge as golf balls. My heart pounded. I could hear it in my ears, head and chest. I just sat back and said to myself, "This bitch has given me herpes." As time went on, it got worse.

The pain became unbearable. I didn't know who to turn to. My family? My friends? God? Now, I know that would have been the smart choice. But at the time, I didn't have a clue. So I called a friend, Telma.

To this day, I feel like she is one of the angels that the Lord sent down to help and watch over me.

Angel; see I am sending an angel before you to protect you on your Journey and lead you safely to the place I have prepared for you.

Exodus 23:20.

The Colors of My Wings

Telma and I had been friends 4 years. Telma had always been my voice of reason, so I called her and told her what I thought was going on with my body. Just as if it was yesterday, I could here her calm voice asking;

"Zanetta, what are you going to do?" "Nothing. What do you mean?"

"Baby, you need to see a doctor right away." I said, "No."

"Zanetta, I'm taking you to somebody's doctor, even if I have to drag you."

Now Telma is not exactly a little chick if you know what I mean, size wise. In fact she is 6 feet and three inches tall; I'm barely five feet, three inches. I thought to myself, I guess I'd better walk instead of being dragged to the doctor's office. Sure enough, I had herpes. It felt like my world had just ended. This confirmed my fears and I began to cry. I looked over at Telma and said, "I don't get it, I'm 21 years old and I have never had unprotected sex with a man. Hell, I had only been with two guys at that point in my life and now this…now I have an STD (sexually transmitted disease) to deal with and on top of me having issues with my sexuality. What will life really be like for me with all this going on? I have so many issues with being molested and so many issues with who I am and what I want that it's no joke. I thought to myself, no man is ever going to want me. No man is ever going to want to deal with me and my mess.

Snare

About a year after contracting herpes, I dealt with absolutely no one. I could not bring myself to do it. Although now when I look back on it, the prognosis of herpes was actually a blessing because it could've been worse. All I know is that I wouldn't let anyone get close to me or even touch me. I was so afraid that I was going to give somebody something or someone was going to give me something far worse.

Something far worse than herpes, something that was more than life altering. Something more along the lines of life threatening. But as time passed my fear of the "far worse" soon was placed in the back of my mind because, I eventually began dating again.

The Colors of My Wings

5

Tangled

By this time I had moved from Georgia to Jacksonville, Florida, I was still in school and still confused. I was confused about everything that was going on in my life. When I moved to Jacksonville there was this younger guy who became hell bent on trying to date me. He was funny, charming, and down to earth. But he was a dude, which made me very hesitant about dating him.

I was hesitant for several reasons. For starters, I had issues with my sexuality. How do I tell this man that I might be bisexual or lesbian? And how do I mention that I have an STD; not life threatening but something I couldn't get rid of? I just didn't know how to discuss it, so I kept him at bay because of my fears.

The Colors of My Wings

Snare

Eventually, he did something stupid and I ran the opposite direction. Once he was out of the way, I began dating another female. This was the first woman that I dated with a child. She was a mother who had been in an abusive relationship.

She was in this abusive union before she and I were introduced. So me being me, I tried to do all things right, of course, and I tried to make her happy. We were dating and about five months into our relationship, yup, she cheated, and not only did she cheat, but she cheated with a man. I came home from school, cleaning up, while she was at work. I cleaned the whole house, cooked dinner, washed and folded clothes. While I cleaning the room, I found a condom wrapper on the floor, under the bed. So I just sat down on the bed in the state of shock or dismay.

I picked up the wrapper and put it on top of the dresser and I sat down again and I waited. I waited until she got home. When she walked in the door I

The Colors of My Wings

simply asked, "Do you have something you need to tell me?"

She grinned and said no, so I let her walk through the house even passing the condom wrapper on the dresser that was in plain view. I wondered did she see this or is she playing stupid, blind or what, so I asked again, "Do you have something you need to tell me?" Again she said, "No, what are you talking about?" So, I got the wrapper and sat it on the table in front of her; her mouth just dropped. I was so pissed I wanted to punch her in the mouth. How could she betray me like that especially after knowing what I had already been through? For whatever it was worth, she did it. Always remember that man will let you down, sometimes they mean to and sometimes they don't, there is only one that will never hurt you, never let you down, and that's God. He might not come when you want him to come but he is always on time. God is always on point.

The Colors of My Wings

Disappointment and this hope will not lead to disappointment. For we know how dearly God loves us, because he has given us the Holy Sprit to fill our hearts with his love.

Romans 5:5

Now I could've either walked away or stayed, but me being me, I stayed and tried to work things out. But it was never the same. Betrayal is one of the hardest pills to swallow. Believe me I have tried, time after time.

Time went on and again little things started to happen. Her phone calls were less and less frequent and eventually stop coming. That's when I decided to pop up for a visit. Let's be clear, a surprise visit. On this particular night I came home from school, about twelve in the morning, when I knocked on the door I was expecting someone to be there with her. But there was no one. I thought maybe I was tripping.

Then about three am there was a knock on the door and I looked at her and she looked at me and I said, "Go answer your door", and she said, "No." So

The Colors of My Wings

I got up and answered the door and at the door was her daughters' father, the same man that had beaten the crap out of her in the past. We discovered that she was lying to both of us about our perspective places in her life. At that moment, I wanted to leave but I couldn't because I had to wait until the morning to take the bus back to Jacksonville.

So I decided to leave the house an go get a drink, hoping this man would be gone by the time I got back, but that would have been too easy. When I got back he wasn't gone. So I balled up on the sofa and drank my drink and fell asleep. But I was to uncomfortable and couldn't quite sleep, because every time I opened my eyes , saw something new and different going on.

These two were having sex in the living room right in front of me. So I tried to sleep harder. But to no avail, sleeping was impossible. So finally morning came. I woke up and noticed two were naked on the floor beside me.

She then she got up and tried to kiss me on my mouth; it took everything in me not to knock fire from this deranged female. Needless to say, I disappeared.

The Colors of My Wings

6

Bait and Switch

As time went on, I eventually started dating again and ended up with a crush on a friend of mine, a friend that had a man. I kept it quiet for the longest time. But we had a mutual friend that I would talk to and I expressed my feelings to this mutual "friend."

She suggested to me that maybe I should tell her my feelings, but she had a man and I didn't even know if she was into women or not.

So one day we all were in the process of getting ready for a party. I went down to her room and she wasn't quite ready. I sat on the bed as she curled her hair. She had on this skirt that had two splits one on each side and she was wearing the heck out of that skirt. I couldn't keep my eyes to myself. Instead of giving myself away, I went outside to wait. Finally, we made it to the party I danced and she sat; I danced and she sat, so then I asked "Why are you

The Colors of My Wings

sitting down at a party?"

She just said, ", I don't know how to dance." So I said okay and I got up and walked around. As I was standing by myself all of a sudden I hear this female voice began to whisper in my ear.

"Zanetta, I've never been with a woman, but I'm so attracted to you."

I said, "Stop playing with me."

"Zanetta, I'm not playing." And then she said, "Zanetta, you have never disrespected me and we have been friends for a long time and if I were ever going to be with a woman it would have to be you," this was a surprise to me, I didn't know how to respond

Snare

so I just walked off. By this time, the buzz that I had was wearing off. I sat down in another area of the party and suddenly her boyfriend appears. When he came over to me he said, "Zanetta I know you want her."

The Colors of My Wings

Snare

I tried to ignore him but he kept pushing so I tried to lie about it. Besides, I felt like he was just trying to find out if I was a lesbian or not, so I denied it for about the first three times he said it to me.

Then he said, "Zanetta, I know you want her. What if you could have her, she might try anything once."

"Okay, what if I do want her?"

"Like I said, she might try anything once." "Well okay, yeah I want her, so now what?"

Zanetta, you can have her", he replied.

Now, I knew that this was too easy for him to just give me a chance at his girl so I wanted to know what the catch was, so I asked him straight up.

"Well, what's the catch?"

"I just want to watch."

Snare

The Colors of My Wings

And once again my dumb behind agreed. But I did this to get close to her. So I went to my room, had another drink, and then I got the call that they were on the way. They picked me up. I went back to their apartment and had some drinks. While I was sipping my drink I was a little nervous because I had never done anything like this before.

To be honest it went down faster than I expected because she took my drink out of my hand and then she grabbed me and pulled me between her legs and she began to kiss me. In that moment I thought I had just lost my mind. It was the way this woman began kissing me. She kissed me like I was her world and then she pulled me on top of her and more and more things began to transpire.

As she and I began having sex her boyfriend watched…well that is for a minute. But before I knew it, he had joined the party. By the time I realized that he had joined in it scared me to death. And I was said to myself,

"What the heck, no, the hell?"

But then I was like, well Zanetta you did this

The Colors of My Wings

to yourself, so deal with it.

The next morning I was like, oh my goodness what did I do? But guess what, I kept doing it for about three months on a regular basis, just because I was infatuated with her. Silly me, I knew we would never be together. So finally, we decided to stop, so we did exactly that, we stopped.

One day I was walking and saw her boyfriend in his car. He pulled over to speak to me and I asked him for a ride back to my dorm room. Not giving it a second thought I jumped in his car because he agreed to give me a lift. At first everything was cool. I felt like we were cool.

But when he missed the turn to get me to my dorm I said, "Where you going?" Rather I asked him. This fool took it upon himself to decide to take me elsewhere. Instead of him dropping me off at my dorm, he decided that he was going to take me home with him. I never realized it but in all that we did he must have been attracted to me. At any rate, when he said we were going to his place I told him, "No, the hell we ain't."

But he wouldn't stop; he started to drive faster. I told

him to pull the car over before I jump out the car while it's moving. So finally he stopped and when he did, I got out the car and walked back to my dorm room. When I got back I called up his girlfriend, which was also my *"friend,"* and told her what had just happened. Now in my mind, I was thinking she was going to talk to her man about his actions, but instead she turned it all back on me. She even accused me of trying to split them up.

I looked at the phone in ill astonishment and was thinking to myself: is she serious? I told her she needed to think back and get real; Try to seriously remember the order of things before you make blanket statements like that. First of all, she came to me; I did not come to her. I mean grant it, I did have a serious thing for her, but at the end of the day, I respected her and kept it to myself. So I told her, "Look if I am not mistaken, you wanted to leave your man for me." And even though I wanted her, I told her not to do it because I couldn't take care of her the way she should be taken care of.

Then she had the nerve to go and tell her roommate what I said about her man and she called her man to see if I was lying about what he had done. First, the

The Colors of My Wings

roommate came knocking on my door to address me on the matter, telling me that I was wrong for informing her of what happened and that I had an ulterior motive. I asked her what the motive was and she cracked her mouth to say I did it because I wanted for myself.

Now granted I did want her, but I didn't have to go to those lengths to get anybody. Like I had said, when she expressed wanting to be with me and drop her dude, I said no to her. But her roommate said, "Even if it were true, Zanetta you shouldn't have told Tammy what happened."

Now by this time, Tammy had come to my room and I'm looking at her like…"Okay, you told me that you didn't want anyone to know our business. So why in the world would you tell your roommate just enough to make me look one kind of way while keeping your three-month fling with me a total secret?" But Tammy had no answer. So, I sat there wondering why Tammy ran and told her roommate who is someone that, according to Tammy, kept drama going. Why would she tell, the drama queen, our business? Well come to find out find out Tammy hadn't told ALL of our business.

The Colors of My Wings

Tammy's roommate didn't know the extent of our three-month escapade. So I turned to Tammy and informed her that I had nothing to hide and that I'd be glad to let her roommate in on the nitty gritty. I could let her know everything that had happened between she, he and me. By this time in the game, I was not exactly hiding my sexuality at all, in fact, I was very open. I mean, I still might not have been sure of who I was in terms of my sexuality, but I was done with hiding.

I never put my business out there but it's not like it was a secret either. However, to the contrary, Tammy didn't want to be open about her desire for women because she was from the Caribbean islands and if her family had found out they would've disowned her flat out. For this very reason I told her to stay with her man, because I couldn't take care of her in the event that her family found out.

I was young. Heck, I was in college, just like her. But our realities were very different. I was totally on my own. The difference between Tammy and me was that her family paid for her college and I paid for mine. So needless to say, after giving careful thoughts to what her roommate might think or say, she told her roommate to leave while we talked it out.

After we talked Tammy called her boyfriend and of course he lied and told her what she wanted to hear and began to threaten my life. To be perfectly clear, he actually invited me to brawl and he threatened to "*chop me up*." And me, being me, I told him do what you got to do. At that point we ended our conversation, I looked at her one last time and then I left.

Later that day, I called up a homeboy of mine and I told him I needed a gun. Did I say that? Yes I said I needed a gun…

Snare

After that threat, I needed this gun for protection. By this time I had called my aunt and told her I was having some issues, but I never went into details. See, I never really said a word to my family about anything unless I felt it needed to be said, but my aunt just somehow knew that there had to be something serious going on for me to call her. Shortly after those two phone calls, my homeboy came back with the gun, suddenly flipped and refused to give it to me.

God

On top of that my aunt called one of my cousins, who lived in Jacksonville. My aunt told my cousin to come and get me.

God

I say this was God because I really and truly was going to do whatever needed to be done to defend my life by any means necessary. But what was so funny is that not too long after that incident, Tammy found out that I wasn't lying to her and that he did try and take me away from the school without my consent.

I bet she regrets talking to her roommate because by this time her roommate had begun spreading rumors over the campus. The rumors were funny as heck because they were about 75% wrong. The word on deck was that yes, Tammy and I had been together, but that I had given her ecstasy.

Ecstasy? Really?" You have got to be kidding me.

The Colors of My Wings

I was like, "For real, ecstasy? That was a lot of pill popping just to have sex, for up to three months! That would be three months worth of ecstasy. Wow! So now I'm a pill popper. What next?" Anyone who knew me knew there was no way that I was going to pop pills, especially after watching my mom the crack addict, depreciate. I don't know what this girl thought she was doing. But Tammy new the truth; she just let the rumors ride and float.

The Colors of My Wings

The Colors of My Wings

7

Test Run

One night I was chilling with my homeboy. We had known each other for about two year by now. By this time, he was not making the best life choices and neither was I for that matter, but he was cool dude. He always seemed to keep it one hundred (which means he kept it real) with me. One night we were hanging out getting our drink on.

Drinking: To Deal with Life

By this time, I had started drinking a quart Old English (malt liquor) and smoking a Black and Mild (cigar) just about every morning at about 10:00 am before I went to class. I did this so I could just chill when I went to class. Now, that didn't include myevening binges. I was just sick of school and sick and tired of being

The Colors of My Wings

sick and tired so I relied on my liquor and cigar to get me through each day.

Something in me said, "I want to see if I still like the wood (sex with men). So, I told my homeboy, that I wanted to have sex. He looked at me and said, "Zanetta, stop playing." "Playing? Playing, who's playing? Do I look like I'm playing? I am so serious right about now. I want to see if I still like men."

He didn't believe me; he knew I was into women. Keep in mind, this is the same guy that attempted to date me 2-yrs before, but because of everything I was dealing with I didn't date him; but never the less here I was piling more of my junk on top of his junk, which basically is the same thing that I had previously said I didn't want to do but we attempted anyway.

Note, at that time I had not been with a man in over two and a half years. I hadn't dealt with that many men anyway. So we tried. But because I hadn't been with a guy in so long it took a minute for him to penetrate me. I was determined to do this, so I didn't give in or try to change my mind. Finally he did it, but then he just picked me up and moved me out of the way and said, "Zanetta, I can't take it, its too wet." I said to myself, "Well I thought that was a good thing?"

So we sat for a minute and then he said, "Ok let's try again," I said, "Okay." But once again he stopped and said again, "Zanetta, I can't do it."

So I said ok, whatever. We stopped and that was that. I kept drinking. Now keep in mind that I had never had unprotected sex with a man until this point. So from that point on we slept together a few times using condoms. But I always had my vice, my drink (liquor); it seemed like the only thing that could help me make an attempt to have sex with a dude, because just the thought of it made me sick to my stomach, but it was something that I wanted do so I just did it.

At this point I only had about eight months of school left before I graduated, even though I had been in college on a basketball scholarship, I had decided to join the Army because after junior college I attended a HBC (historically black college) school I only received a

The Colors of My Wings

partial scholarship; most HBC's did not offer full rides due to funding. So I used multiple student loans to cover my tuition, housing and meal plans; I didn't have anyone helping me pay for my college education.

I paid for it the best way I knew how. And now that I was almost finished with school I had to figure out how I was going to pay the piper, the United States Government. I thought long and hard about the best way to approach the pay back. So, I decided to get out debt by joining the United States Army. In preparation for the Army, my recruiter took me to the meps station to complete a battery of test. When the doctor came in he said, "Everything is fine Miss Collins, except for the fact that you are pregnant."

I quickly responded, "No, I'm not."

In total disbelief I decided to get a second opinion. I went straight to the clinic and got tested again. The results of the second test provided relieving news, "Miss Collins you can calm down; you're fine, you're not pregnant."

That was music to my ears, it was a well of melodies and harmonies that made me feel relieved. I felt relieved.

The Colors of My Wings

There was no way Zanetta could possibly be pregnant! So, as time went by I started paying attention to things I had not really been paying attention to before. For starters my body didn't feel right. I just felt off, so to speak. Another thing; my breasts were tender and sore. But that was normal for me during certain times of the month; Within a week or so of my cycle, my breast would be sore and tender to touch so, that was nothing new, but I just still felt different. So I told a close friend about this crazy scare and she suggested I take another test. Her words were along the lines of, "Zanetta, you might want to take another test, just to make sure. It can get tricky in the beginning"

So I took another test and low and behold it came up positive. Me, pregnant? Yes! I immediately called home and told my mom. At first she didn't believe; Hell, I didn't believe it myself but the reality of it all was that I *was having a baby*. Soon I returned back home to Cocoa and took another test just to be sure. Of course, the results had not changed, Zanetta was having a baby!

God

The Colors of My Wings

As I laid across my grandmother's bed I pondered how and when did had happened. Jerry and I had sex maybe 4 times. The only time we didn't use a condom was the first time and I didn't really count that because keep in mind, we really didn't have sex the first time because he couldn't take it. Also, after the first time we always used a condom. I thought to myself, " I guess I need to tell him." So, I called Jerry and told him I was pregnant. I was shocked to find out that this did not seem to shock him. I guess he knew that he slipped or something, and this was confirmed in his next sentence.

"Well I'm not surprised."

Now when this joker said this to me, instantly my mind began to race.

"Huh? What do you mean?" "You knew?"

"Well I kind of figured you might be."

I was lost. I wasn't getting it. So again I asked him "Like what in the devil do you mean by saying that you *kind of* knew?"

The Colors of My Wings

"Well…the first time we had sex, I ejaculated." Still stuck on stupid, I asked him, "When did *that* occur, because I don't remember *any* of this."

"Oh crap!"

I grabbed my mouth in shock. Even though I didn't get it at the time, and not up until that moment, in retrospect when he said he couldn't do it, (have sex with me) it was because he had already ejaculated. "You're too wet."

He must have been scared to tell me. All this time, I never knew that he had ejaculated before we could even get started. I guess he hoped that nothing happened or went wrong. So, I reminded him that we stopped the first time and nothing happened. His rebuttal was, "Yeah, we stopped, but I got stuck and I ejaculated."

Still looking crazy in the face, I tried to sort through all the details. "But Jerry, you were only in there about 2.5 seconds. So what do you mean you got stuck?"

Then this man said to me, "Zanetta, well to be honest I didn't worry about it because I figured I smoke too much weed to make a baby." I blurted out, "Oh Lord, what have I gotten myself into? You could have at least told me that you came inside of me, because honestly I really and truly had no idea."

And we know that God causes everything to work together for the good of those who love God and are called according to his purpose for them.

Rom 8:28

He then gave me this nice spiel about wanting to be better than his father was toward him, but of course that never happened.

Ohhhh-kay, let's not go there.

So, after finding out about my pregnancy, I weighed my options. I briefly thought of having an abortion, but I just couldn't do it. So now I had to step up, screw my head back on straight, and get my head back in school. I also had to continue to work and graduate. Especially, since the military was not an option at this point. My schedule was rough. Every Monday morning I rode the bus north and walked a mile to my internship. I worked from 8:00 am to 5:00 pm, then walked the mile back and got the bus. Once I got to school, I would go to class from 6:00 pm until 8:30 pm. Then every Tuesday through Sunday, I walked to the bus station and headed south to the mall where I worked from 10:00 am until 2:00 pm.

When I got off work I got back on the bus and headed back to the school from 4:00 pm until 8:30 pm, Tuesday through Thursday, on top of the fact I worked weekends. Now if you can imagine all this, picture it with me pregnant. I did this, day after day, until I was about seven months pregnant. It's not surprising that the doctor put me on bed rest in the middle of the seventh month. Determined not to lose hope or give up I brought all of my schoolwork home and the last week of school I came back to complete my exams.

After turning in my exams, I got my hair braided and began packing so I could head back to Cocoa. At that point I was full with emotions; I felt as though so much had happened in so little time, it was crazy! As I began packing I felt something pop. "What in the heck?," You guessed it, I was in labor. I went to the hospital right away; there was no turning back. I actually began to feel excited about having my baby.

The Colors of My Wings

After my son came into the world, instantly I knew that God had sent me my baby. He was my blessing. He helped save my life. He gave me new meaning in life, a new reason for living. When I look back I see the hand of God and his grace over everything.

After all was said and done I graduated one week after giving birth to De'Vyon. It was hard but, by God's grace, I did it.

The Colors of My Wings

8

Be All You Can Be

As they say, once another task is down, another task begins. After I graduated, I returned to my hometown. My mother and I decided to move into an apartment together. She was clean from her drug addiction and I had no plans on settling in Brevard County, at least not for the long haul. So our move was sufficient for the time being. The long and short of it is that I got a job and about a year later, I did join the Army to get out of debt and also start a new life, but I still had issues with my sexuality, issues about my child hood, issues about my life, just issues, issues, issues across the board.

After joining the military I came to realize that they had some pretty strong unspoken policies such as, "*The Don't Ask, Don't Tell*, rule about people and their sexuality, which I tried to abide by.

For me, this worked out. Heck, I even had my "play-play" marriage, as I called it, so minding my business was

The Colors of My Wings

not an issue. I had gotten married so that I didn't have to give up custody of my son. My son was and is my world and there was no way I was going to give him up. Getting married was the perfect cover for me or so I thought but the fact still remained, I was still "*gay*".

But it didn't work out that way because Chris got into trouble fighting, which was against the rules. As a soldier, I couldn't have any trouble like that around me. In the military, this is considered inexcusable so, he had to go.

Chris and I had a deal and which was for him not to bring any drama my way, our plan was blown when he began fighting so he had to kick rocks.

I had good reasons for joining the military, but after a while, it just wasn't cutting it for me. Yes, I love my country, but I love my son more. I refused to get sent to war and leave my son alone at home; his father wasn't around and I didn't want anyone else raising my child.

After Chris moved out, I continued with my life, my military career, and reluctantly my battle with my sexuality.

The Colors of My Wings

At first, my education, lifestyle, and the military did not conflict with each other, but that quickly changed and ultimately caused me to make a life changing decision.

I have never been a secretive person and if I cared about someone, I openly showed affection…PROBLEM! The entire time I was in the Army, I found the people in charge to be foul and shady; they were not trustworthy at all. They were either trying to sleep with me or degrade me in some way…PROBLEM! I really felt that because I was an educated black woman I didn't receive any respect…PROBLEM! It seemed they looked down on you if you didn't start at the bottom of the ladder and worked you way up to the top. But it wasn't my fault that I had entered the military with a degree. So reluctantly, after deep consideration, I decided to get out of the armed services.

Before being released from the military, I had several jobs lined up as well as plans to return to school for a second degree, but because they took so long releasing me, the job opportunities were given to someone else. And as far as school was concerned, that backfired because I could not get the approval to attend dental hygiene school because I already had a degree. I thought as a disabled I thought as a disabled veteran I would have support, but they still turned me down. Now I understand it; it was not my time. What I have come to learn now is that things are not done in our time, but in God's timing for our lives. My father had a bigger and better plan for my life. I thought I had things mapped out and figured out, but my plans failed. No military, no school, and no job meant that I had to go back to the drawing board.

Working hard is what I have always done so I returned to doing what I did best, which was to work with a fury. I landed two jobs. One was as a pizza delivery driver during the day and the other was cleaning a local hospital at night. My son and I lived with my mother, brother-in-law, sister, and set of twins. We slept on a blow up air mattress; I did what I had to do to survive. I had to survive; I had to make a way for my son and me.

The Colors of My Wings

Eventually, I got my own apartment, which for me, was my personal serenity quarters. I spent most of my time alone just thinking, planning and praying. That was the second time that I had attempted to ask God to remove this spirit off me, but it never seemed to happen for me, the spirit of homosexuality. However, faith without works is room for destruction. I tried to walk away but it just never happened for me.

I fully expect many to argue, "Some people have faith; others have good deed." But I say, "How can you show me your faith if you don't have good deeds." You say you have faith, for you believe that there is one God." Good for you. Even the demons believe this, and they tremble in terror. How foolish. Can't you see that faith without good deeds is useless? Don't you remember that our ancestor Abraham was shown to be right with God by his actions when he offered his son Isaac on the altar? You see, his faith and his actions worked together. His actions made so it happened just as the

The Colors of My Wings

scriptures say: "Abraham believed God, and God counted him as righteous because of his faith." "He was even called the friend of God." So you see, we are shown to be right with God by what we do, not by faith alone. Rehab the prostitute is another example. She was shown to be right with God by her actions when she hid those messages and sent them safely away by a different road.' Just as the body is dead without breath,'' so also faith is dead without works.

James 2:18-26.

So, then I said to myself, "Well hey I asked and nothing happened so I'm going to do me." And I did just that, I lived my life as I saw fit, because nothing seem to change. But I know now that,

The race is not given to the swift, but to those who endurth to the end, inspired by,

The Colors of My Wings

Ecclesiastes 9:11,

I have observed something else under the sun. The fastest runner doesn't always win the race, and the strongest warrior doesn't win the battle. The wise sometimes go hungry, and the skillful are not necessarily wealthy. And those who are educated don't always lead by chance, by being in the right place at the right time.

The Colors of My Wings

9

Wild Card

Why is love so frustrating? I mean I felt like, heck, I'm a good person. I work hard. I have a huge heart and I will give anything for those I love. So what am I missing?

By now, I had a few relationships that ultimately were dead ends. Not only were these failed relationships dead ends; they were painful pitfalls. Not that I want to kick-start a "why me" saga or anything but why couldn't I find someone that shared an ounce of what I call selflessness in a relationship? I couldn't totally give up on love, because we all need love, right?

So here we go again. I began dating this chick that seemed to be sooooooooooooo into "church". We spent all of our spare time together; she always spoke about her love for the Lord, and said she didn't want to be a lesbian or a homosexual. I asked her why she was with me, but she couldn't answer the question. Actually she didn't want to deal with me because she knew it wasn't right. So, I respected her wishes and attempted to remove myself from her life. However, once I was gone, she would come back, "Zanetta don't go."

"Well, you don't want me or this lifestyle, so why are you doing this?"

"I don't want to be without you."

Could you believe this? That circle of "goodbyes" and "don't goes" continued for a while – until I got completely tired of the emotional roller coaster.

"Ok! Enough is enough."

I didn't want to deal with her emotional and confusing ride any longer. I didn't want it anymore. Enough was enough. I was sick of bending over for people; it was just never enough. Takers – Our God is a jealous God; he doesn't want you to put anything or anyone before him.

> *So all of us who have had that veil removed can see and reflect the glory of the Lord. And the Lord – who is the Spirit – makes us more and more like him as we are changed into his glorious image.*

The Colors of My Wings

2 Corinthians 3:18

We as a people tend to put trust and faith in things that are tangible. We trust in things we can see and feel not what we can't see or touch. But what we fail to realize is that things that are tangible also come with an expiration date. The tangible item will die, spill, or break – every relationship or situation that is not ordained by God. This was hard for me.

After my relationship with "the church girl" I became bitter. I didn't care about the feelings of others nor how I treated them. I had made up my mind about what I wanted and was going to be. Why should I allow what happened to me in my past dictate what happens in my future? So, I began dating three females at one time.

None of these females knew about the other. My attitude was: why should they know about one another? After all, I wasn't serious with any of them.

Hurt People, hurt people…

The Colors of My Wings

I had become inwardly nasty from being hurt. One of the females I was seeing assumed that because I was nice to her, I wanted to be in a relationship with her. Wrong! I tried to explain to her and make it very clear that I didn't want a relationship. To make it very clear, one night after sex, my phone rang. I answered it right in front of her like she wasn't there. It was the woman I knew I was going to eventually end up with because we had something special.

After I got off the phone, Kim wanted to know who I had been talking to. I was more than happy to fill her in. It was Veronica. I told Kim how special Veronica was too me and I watched her confidence crumble like breadcrumbs at the bottom of the loaf. What was I thinking? I was just playing around with these chicks until I got a chance to start a relationship with Veronica.

Once Veronica and I began spending time together and we discussed the possibly of us beginning a relationship, I thought of moving to her hometown because there were more jobs available down there verses Brevard County. But she wanted to get her son away from there; he had begun getting into trouble. I agreed. If that's what she wanted, I was fine with whatever choice she made. After that, everything fell into place. I was getting what I asked for: a family.

Veronica made the move, I got a better job, and we moved into our own home. It was nice as heck. We had a beautiful three-bedroom home with two bathrooms on a split–level floor plan with a two-car garage on a corner lot. I loved the Florida room; it was my sanctuary. I felt like the Jefferson's. We were moving on up. Then suddenly, a deep- rooted fear gripped Veronica. It was like, "Oh my God; I just walked away from everything for this female, what if something goes wrong?"

Out of nowhere, Veronica grew bitter and became hateful toward me. Every time I turned around a new argument about the same things would present itself. I didn't understand it. I did my best to take care of her, her kids, my son, and myself – why am I getting her butt to kiss? I understood that part of it was because she couldn't find the type of job she wanted and I didn't fuss about that. I just tried to be supportive and be who and what I thought she needed at that time, but my thoughts were not making things better.

The Colors of My Wings

Nothing I did mattered. The arguments never stopped. The fighting got worse. Every other day it was an accusation of some sort..."You're cheating." If she wasn't accusing me of cheating, she was implying that I treated my son better than I treated her daughters..."Why don't my girls have what De'Vyon has?"

I was like, "What"? So, I did everything in my power to please her, over compensating, trying to please. Then it turned into..."I'm leaving, I'm leaving, I'm leaving."

I got to my breaking point and said, "Then leave." I have never been one to beg a soul. At the end of the day, I can do bad all by myself.

Once I realized the fussing wasn't going to stop, I said to myself: Well, okay, I can fix this real quick. I'll move into a cheaper place just in case Veronica decides to leave. This way I would be in a better situation for my son and me. So we moved back to Cocoa, from Palm Bay Florida. We moved into another three-bedroom home with one full bathroom and a powder room. Not so bad at all. We even had a pool. It wasn't in the best neighborhood but it was decent living.

Veronica had a string of small jobs and because of our frustrations our sex life had dwindled to nothing. In her mind I should have been the one to initiate the intimacy in our relationship. I've always figured a relationship is a two-way street, even in the bedroom. A lot of times I felt like I worked, I cooked, I cleaned, the least she could do was take the initiative in our bedroom, but I couldn't get that either.

I reached the point where I felt like I couldn't win on either end of the stick. I didn't go anywhere and I didn't do anything, but there was always a complaint, I was unhappy. I told Veronica that I didn't want to be with her anymore. I was tired of trying; I didn't want to try anymore.

Then one morning I was on my way to work and my phone rang. "Hey, Zanetta, your girl was in a bad accident." This really blew my mind; the crazy part was that I was on Highway US–1 and she was on Fiske and we were both heading south in about the same position with only one road between us – we were at the same point, but on different streets. I rushed to the scene of the accident. I was a nervous wreck. My hands were sweating. My heart was racing. I was just out of it. A car had run the light and hit a truck. The truck spun around and caused a wrench to fly out of its tailgate, through the car window and hit Veronica in the ribs. The craziest part is Veronica wasn't even a part of the accident but ended up the only person seriously injured. She was hurt badly; she had broken two ribs.

After Veronica was dismissed we had to stay at my grandmother's house because she had to have care 24/7 and I had to work. When we got there, something wasn't right. Veronica wasn't breathing right. "Veronica, let's go. I'm taking you back to the hospital."

We went back to the hospital to get a second opinion. All the left side ribs were shattered; and she had a punctured lung. It blew my mind that they had sent her home in the first place. But if that's not shocking enough, they did it again. They claimed that there was nothing they could do for her; she just needed to rest. I was pissed off. What in the heck were we going to do with her in this fragile state?

With no other option we reluctantly headed back

home. This was a serious situation; taking care of Veronica. Between my grandmother and myself, we bathed her, took her to the bathroom, and fed her. I did this even though we were not together anymore. I did it until one night she climbed on top of me and asked me if we could work things out. But I said no. There was no way I could go back to loving her after the hell she put me through, especially when I gave her my all. She blew that opportunity.

After that I began to pull away even further. I wanted her to hate me. I tried to make myself undesirable, but no matter what I did or didn't do, she still wanted to be in a relationship with me. But the fact still remained even though we were not together anymore we were still living together because we still had a lease.

So one day I thought: Well maybe, I'm wrong. Maybe I should try. I asked her if we could work things out; she reluctantly said yes. So we tried again, for about two and a half months, during which I frequently asked myself: Zanetta why, why are you putting yourself through this? Also, during this period, and throughout the course of our relationship, I was also very sick. I was dealing with

The Colors of My Wings

various issues. I had fibroid tumors that were causing me excessive pain and grief. I had no energy. I was losing so much blood; it seemed like every other day between her health, my health, and the kid's health the toll was stacked against us.

So, I decided that I had to be true to myself. I could not fake the funk. I told her I couldn't do it anymore; that I was done. I had completely fallen out of love with Veronica. But the strangest thing was that I still loved her with all my heart and desperately wanted to be back in love with her, but it just wasn't going to happen.

Veronica finally got a job, and we decided to move out of our house because I refused to sign another lease with her. Why create commitment connections when we both knew that this was a dead-end situation? Weighing our options, we decided to move in with my mother until she got on her feet and I had surgery.

Eventually, I had my surgery to remove my tumors, but prior to it I met this young lady by the name of Tina. At the time, Veronica and I had been apart for about six months, even though we still shared the same address. Tina and her ex had been apart about the same amount of time by the time as well. While I recovered, Veronica struggled with the kids and what I needed done. For that very reason I asked her not to come back to Tampa while I was in the hospital. I was frustrated with her and honestly I really wanted Tina there anyway. Tina had the ability to just relax me, I mean completely. I wasn't sure if she would come or not? Surprisingly Tina came to visit me in the hospital all the way from Orlando.

That was like a one-hour drive. Tina even stayed with me in the hospital. We both seemed to be at a place in our lives where for the both of us…this was it. If we were going to try a relationship – yet again – and discovered that it didn't work, we were both done, completely, with relationships and women period.

The time spent between Tina and I felt so right. I even began to think of marriage and that was a new place for me; I had never sincerely thought of marring a woman. I basically felt that everyone I loved would not agree to such a promise. Marriage was a serious thing and

The Colors of My Wings

in this relationship I seriously could see this. I could see us spending the rest of our lives together. I never wanted the day that was suppose to be the happiest day of my life to be tainted with hate, frustration, and misunderstanding. I put that out of my mind until Tina came into my life.

Nevertheless, the thoughts were there; the thoughts were strong. I even wrote my vows, picked the wedding colors and checked into locations. We had a great relationship. But all of a sudden the ex girlfriend – oh my bad ex-wife – yes I said "ex-wife", popped back up. She figured Tina had moved on with her life and wanted her back. All of a sudden, confusion set in for Tina, feelings surfaced that Tina didn't realize were still inside her. She didn't know what to do or how to handle the situation. I could have respected her more if she had just said, "Zanetta, I'm confused."

But instead, even after me asking repeatedly, "Tina, are you sure that you want this relationship?" she kept me in the dark. I was trying to be the bigger person; be supportive of the situation, you know?

The whole while, she kept professing her love for me.

The Colors of My Wings

Even then something just wouldn't settle; something didn't feel right. I knew I was going to end up being hurt, but I still stood by her. And then, she ended our relationship over a text message.

I was devastated. I didn't understand. It hurt me to the core. Before her, I never wanted to love again. Loving people never seemed to get me anywhere but back in the hot seat with pain, hurt and tears. Every time, and in every scenario, I faced more pain; with every sacrifice another hole in my heart.

I even broke down in front of my mother. My mother, although I'm sure she has felt my pain with different relationships, could probably count on one hand the number of times she ever saw me cry. But the catch was I think my mother felt as if I was crying over Tina, but in actuality it was so much deeper than just Tina. Don't get me wrong, that was a part of it, but the bigger issue was me.

Zanetta was my deepest problem.

I didn't understand what I was doing wrong. I didn't understand why I kept getting caught up in these circles. I just didn't get it. It got to the point that all I

The Colors of My Wings

did was cry. I cried so much it was as if I was purging from my history of brokenness and wounds. I would cry in the bed, cry on the floor, I would cry in the car for hours on end, hour after hour after hour just so my son wouldn't see me cry. I would even cry in the shower so that no one could see my tears. I would be balled up on the floor of the tub or on my knee just asking God, why me? I couldn't eat. I couldn't sleep. Whenever I tried to eat I would vomit. Between my surgery and the stress, I lost more than twenty pounds.

Finally, it was time for me to head back to work. I tried to be positive about life, hope, truth and my future. I figured that work would help clear my mind. At the time I didn't realize how far gone I was. But when the devil is busy, he is exactly that, busy. I guess he didn't realize – that my father had a plan for me. Sucker!

My first day back to work I received a phone call. It was my mother, crying her heart out. She was so upset, I could barely make out her words. My cousin was dead. I just stopped. I tried to hold it together. I knew I was holding on to what little strength I had left by the skin of my teeth and if that string broke, it would be the end. But I couldn't hold back. I just broke down, right where I was.

Needless to say, once again I was out of work. By the time I got home my mom was crying unbearably. The cops informed us that they actually found my cousin almost two years ago in the Indian River. They couldn't identify the body because it was so severely decomposed; even the pigment in her skin was missing. She had been listed in the paper as a Caucasian woman. I was in utter shock. We always hoped for a happy ending; for her return.

At this point, I felt as if I was hanging on to the little sanity that I had remaining by the skin of my chin and again the enamel on my teeth. After getting a grip on my grief. I decided to return to work. Upon my return, I clocked in and prepared to do my work as usual. Then I was called to the manager's office.

"Zanetta, we are going to have to let you go."

Hell, life was so rough on me that I nearly thanked them for it. In fact the only thing I had to say was, "I wish you guys had called me before I came to work this morning." That's just how gone I was. I didn't even care anymore. The only thing I wanted was sleep. I didn't want to deal with anything. Not a job. Not money. Not even family. Hell, I didn't want to deal with me. I was just done. So I did just that, I slept. And slept. And slept. Morning. Noon. Night.

My sister asked me what I was going to do? I answered, nothing, primarily because I didn't care. I'd been working since I was fourteen and needed a break. Furthermore, I just didn't care anymore.

The Colors of My Wings

10

Fire and Desire

Maybe this was a sign. A good sign. Maybe my desire to just do something meant that I was ready to breathe again. Who knows? All I know is that I got on my computer one day and an old friend found me. Jasmine was a former teammate I played basketball with. We began talking on the regular basis. She was married with three kids; I was just chilling, not expecting or searching for anything. I was so done with everything and everybody. She had never been with a woman and was very much into her kids and she loved the Lord. We became pretty close. We became so close that at first we didn't even notice the turn that our relationship taken. Needless to say we began spending time with each other and eventually things began to happen on their own.

The Colors of My Wings

Snare

Her husband was never home. She knew he had cheated on her more than once. As a matter of fact they hadn't had sex in over a year.

Snare

We talked every day. Jasmine let me know just how lonely she was, how betrayed and unloved she felt. I reassured her that she was a dynamic mother, a wonderful person, and a beautiful woman. I could sense that she clung onto those words and needed to hear them. She felt empty, drained and abandoned. After a while, it became obvious that there was an unspoken attraction between she and I. The energy was fire. Suddenly I became the person that filled that void in her life; a placeholder for her husband. He should have been spending time with Jasmine and the kids but instead we did all the things he never did. It was not difficult to waltz right into her life because of the hole he blew into her heart. So I became

The Colors of My Wings

the person filling that void; a void he should never have created.

He should have been loving who God gave him and spend quality time with her, and make sure she knew she came first. We did all the things that he never did: making love to the simplest of things like sharing a glass of wine in the midst of a foot rub. I just paid attention and gave her what she needed and deserved.

Her kids were involved in track and field. Although it looked like the perfect family activity, since her husband was a professional coach, it was not. He treated her like she was invisible. He never attended any of the instate track meets, but went to the out of state to make sure his kids excelled. One particular weekend, I knew he and the kids had to go out of town for a competition, which made it perfect for us to spend time alone. My phone rang…"Hey Z, just wanted to let you know that the coast was clear."

That was my sign to hit the road. I grabbed my gear and my gadget named Marcus and I made sure my waves were tight and my cologne was right and I was out. I could hear the desire in her voice; I swear I could feel

The Colors of My Wings

electricity through the phone. I had to have her. I was open. I would have bet my bottom dollar that she was so ready for me. Her house was a 2-½ hour drive away from mine. I was there in what seemed like ninety minutes. I didn't stop to pee, nor did I need a GPS to find her.

Finally I arrived at her house. Being shy, I gave her a quick hug so not to be forceful. But when I embraced her I got a whiff of her perfume. She smelled so good. We sat down on the sofa under a dim light and shared a glass of wine. I told her how nice her blouse was, and then stroked her hair. That alone was nice. It was special. I took off her heels and began to rub her feet. I worked my way up her leg and began caressing her inner thigh. Although this was her first experience with a woman, it was clear we both knew the meaning of my visit.

There was an unspoken truth in that moment: she wanted me as much as I wanted her. The kiss that we shared was so hot and heavy that she began to tremble. We moved towards the bedroom. I knew this was the bed her husband slept in, the bed they had created three kids in, but I didn't care; I was going to give her what she deserved – a night with Rico my alter ego.

The Colors of My Wings

You see, me, I am really shy when it comes to intimacy. But Rico, he was different; he was the Tiger in me. Our first night together I didn't even need Marcus, Marcus was my strap on. Instead of that, I just went to town. As our evening ended, we fell asleep in each other arms. And that's how we woke up.

After time passed, and happiness grew, the ole hubby got an itch about me. He became suspicious. He just knew something was going on between Jasmine and me. She was cheating.

You must not commit adultery,
Exodus 20:14

Jasmine's husband began to ask her what was going on between us: were we in a relationship? She said no and told him we were just friends. Which was true. It just wasn't the entire truth. We were much, much more.

So one day while she was at work, he called the house to talk to me. He asked if something was going on between us? I lied and said no. I hung up and felt frustrated; senses grew: hatred towards him, the entire situation – I had lied. It wasn't my place to tell him; it was Jasmine's. I wondered when she would step up and tell him about us – or at least what she led me to believe about us. He expressed his feelings about the issue. He rather Jasmine slept with his best friend rather than to discover he was losing his wife to a woman. During our conversation, he said that if I was the personal Jasmine was having an affair, I would have a problem. I asked what was he insinuating. I asked him if he was threatening me. He said no. But it was an open-ended threat. So I just told him straight up: If he had been the father, the husband, and most importantly the man that he should have been for his family, he would've never had to worry about me or anyone else.

"You've got a lot of nerve."

"I sure do. Take Care."

The Colors of My Wings

The Colors of My Wings

11

The Awaking

Father's Day was about to roll around. Jasmine hadn't seen her father in quite some time and she really wanted to see him.

"Jas' how long has it been?"

"About three years."

"Okay, why haven't you seen him in long?"

"It's a ten-hour drive and I can't drive long distances." "What about ole boy?"

"Please, that's like beating a dead horse. I've asked him nearly a hundred times and he always has an excuse."

"Like what?"

"No money, no time, not in the mood, I'll be away on business, you name it".

He just never made time to take me."

"It's cool. I got you. Pick a

The Colors of My Wings

weekend."

So like I said, Father's Day was around the corner and that's when Jasmine wanted to go. She and I headed to North Carolina to see her father, which also gave me an opportunity to meet her brothers.

Surprise. When we got there, I realized I knew one of her brothers. His name was Sheldon McCray Sr. He had become a preacher. He even had his own church. I wasn't really sure how to act or how the rest of her family would act towards me; even though nothing was said, the adoration and affection that we had towards, one another showed. It was obvious. Nevertheless, her family treated me like family.

As far as Pastor Sheldon, he didn't really say very much. He just observed the situation. As our weekend began to wind down, on a Sunday morning, time came for us to get on the road. We were debating whether or not to go to her brother's church before we left. We didn't want to get on the road too late, and I didn't have any decent clothing to wear. All I had was jeans and a polo shirt.

Even though I was a lesbian, and I was never really the type of female to wear a dress, I still felt like I would

The Colors of My Wings

have rather had heels and slacks. I try to be presentable at all times. We decided to just stick our heads in for a few and head out. But something happened. From the time I walked in those doors – something happened. The young lady began to sing and I began to cry. I cried, and cried, and cried and on the inside I was tripping; I didn't know what I was crying for.

Later the following year, her brother and I were talking. He had been elevated to Apostle by then. At any rate he said to me, "Zanetta, you had what's called an awakening." This now makes perfect sense to me. You see: When God wants you, it doesn't matter where you are, and He will come and get what's his.

For many are called, but few are chosen.

Matthew 22:14

I cried throughout the entire service. Then all of a sudden Apostle McCray called me up to the front of the church. I had never been in front of a church before. He just looked at me and then hugged me and said, "Zanetta, it's going to be okay."

That was all he said. Then he called his sister Jasmine up and told her he knew what was going on between she and I. He told her to make sure she understood the choices that she was making in her life; she should make sure that she was doing it for the right reasons and not out of spite toward her husband. He told her that the devil was out to get her; she had a purpose in life and the devil didn't want her to succeed.

I knew she needed this; she needed it because she was so hurt, so much so that she felt invisible in this world. Then he told her that if she had gotten on the road rather than coming to church, she would've gotten killed. God had a bigger purpose for her life.

The next thing I saw was Jasmine gagging and choking and coughing and crying. Then she began to vomit during service. They were praying over her. She sat down next to me and something was different, very different. We both felt it. Once service was over they asked for all visitors to stand. I stood up and informed them that it was nice to be in the house of the Lord where

The Colors of My Wings

I didn't feel like I was going to burn up by the way people looked at me. We said our good byes and got on the road.

At first there was silence. Then finally we began to talk about the morning's events. I told her I thought she was going to leave me after the service, but she said no. She told me that she wasn't going anywhere. Then she told me that she wouldn't be surprised if I stopped dating women one day. I just laughed and said: If you say so. I'll believe it when I see it. Right now I just don't see it. As we traveled, we saw three accidents that all included a truck. All I could think about was what her brother had said earlier.

By the time we got home we had both made certain choices that would change our lives. Jasmine decided to leave her husband. I decided to give up my apartment. The goal was to be together and we were going to move to North Carolina. Everything was set when all of a sudden, she called me. She was very quiet. She said, "Zanetta, I can't leave." I was like, "What do you mean, you can't leave? " I was pissed. She had decided that she needed to divorce her husband before leaving;

she wanted to be free and clear of everything pertaining to her marriage and to him.

I was like, here we go with the dumb crap. I felt like, do I look stupid to you? Now don't get me wrong, I understood her reasoning for making that choice, but honestly, I wasn't trying to hear it. I felt she wanted to string me along.

I told her that I felt like she wasn't going to leave her husband and I just began to cry. I felt like, here my stupid butt goes again. Then all of a sudden, she began to pray, which was nothing new for us, we often prayed on the phone together, every day as a matter of fact. But she began to pray and the entire time there was one consistent message that stood out for me: to be still. All I kept hearing, feeling and seeing in the spirit were the words "be still".

Be still and know that I am God.
Psalm 46:10

Fortunately, she never told him a thing and I kept my

place in Rockledge, Florida. "Jas' just stayed in Gainesville with her family and to this day they are still together."

The Colors of My Wings

The Colors of My Wings

12

Tired of Being Tired

By this time I began going to church on my own. I visited the 8:00 am service at my aunts' church. I was still in limbo initially with Jas after our last conversation. So one day I just told her that I was done. I told her that she had a lot of things that she had to deal with, and I had my issues as well, so we ended it. I reached the point where enough was enough for me. My heart was pierced but what I didn't know that this time it was God who had pierced it.

I had been contemplating joining my Aunt's church. However, one day, one of my best friends invited me to visit her church service. Telma, one of my closest friends, is truly a Godsend in my life. Telma had been there for me since I was sixteen. I called her up one day just to check in on her and she was like,

"Hey, Z. Why don't you come join me at church?" "Okay, sure, when, what time?"

So I got myself together and went to the Oil of Joy

The Colors of My Wings

Church Ministries. I felt something in that name. I don't know what it was but it kind of caressed my soul. That may sound a little weird, but I felt like God was reaching out to me in so many ways. I knew it was him saying what I needed to hear, showing what I needed to say, and letting me know what I needed to know. I had hardened, so I needed some oil and I was emotionally drained so I needed some joy.

My first visit to Oil of Joy was both strange and interesting at the same time. I say this because I grew up in a Baptist church and this church was nothing like your traditional Primitive Baptist Church. The people in this church spoke in tongues, which had never been my scene, just not my norm, at all. Needless to say, I sat next to Telma. I sat there looking around like, man, what did this chick get me into?

I had never experienced that type of activity in a church before. So after my first visit, they invited me bowling with them.

But the entire time I braced myself for the looks, snickers and comments that I felt were bound to come, but that never happened. So, I bowled and I even had a nice conversation with the pastor. I really enjoyed myself. For once, some good clean fun times and more importantly no judgments, which was the biggest thing for me. They made me feel at home. They made me feel loved despite the fact that I was different. They just loved me and that was the bottom line for me. They loved me.

> *Love ye therefore the stranger: for ye were strangers in the land of Egypt,*
>
> *Deuteronomy 10:19*

So I continued to attend services. On the 3rd Sunday that I attended, sitting there in church, the pastor asked if there was anyone who wanted to testify. I hesitated. The next thing I knew, I was standing. I was the fourth person.

Something just came over me and I stood up to speak. What you need to be very clear about is the fact that this is something that "Zanetta" just doesn't do. I wasn't ashamed of who I was, but because folks looked at me like I was an alien; especially church or religious people. They always judged and to me just being nosey. But I stood anyway. Better yet, I think the Holy Spirit stood me up. I stood up and began to cry. Tears literally flooded down my face. I cried for what seemed like an eternity before I could even open my mouth. I felt like I was about to vomit a baby. Finally, it came out...

> *"I have been a lesbian for 13yrs of my life, and I'm tired."*

To be completely honest, it wasn't only that; there were so many other things that bound me as well.

> *Such as sit in darkness and in the shadow of death, being bound in affliction and iron,*
>
> *Psalms 107:10*

But the only thing people saw was a lesbian. They didn't know I had been struggling with anxiety. They

The Colors of My Wings

didn't know there were days where I couldn't even be in the same room with other people. I didn't want anyone to even come close to me, because I felt like snapping. The closer someone got, the more I lost control. I was suffering from depression. I kept my distance from everyone. I was so fearful that they could see right through me, through this wall I tried to erect piece by piece. I was coming apart. There were times when I went for days, sometimes weeks, without eating or bathing.

I just didn't want to do anything for myself anymore. I wanted to disappear from myself and everyone else for that matter. For months on end I couldn't sleep. I would lay down in bed and try to sleep, but I would wake up every fifteen minutes throughout the night.

I was having night panic attacks. I would look around, expecting someone to break in my house or walk up my stairs at any moment. I was so paranoid that I slept with a knife under my pillow and I always kept my hand on that knife. I just didn't trust anyone, not even my so-called family. I took so many prescription medications that I felt like a zombie. Before I lost my job, I'd been so drugged up that I couldn't function.

But after that day, I called Jasmine. Even though we weren't together any more, we were still close. I said: Well, Jas, I guess you were right. I told her that I stood up in church and testified about being a lesbian and that I was tired and that I didn't want it anymore. She was happy for me. She said, "I told you."

At that moment, I thought about our trip to Greensboro and how on the way back we stopped at her brother's church.

!!!Flashback!!!

"Z, I would not be surprised if you stopped dating women."

Now at the time she said this, I totally blew it off. But suddenly, it was a real consideration. I really wanted out of this lifestyle; I just knew I needed a change because I was just tired. I was tired of being hurt, tired of feeling like a failure, tired of chasing my own tail, going through the same stuff and allowing myself to be in the same old situations over and over again. I needed out.

The Colors of My Wings

The Colors of My Wings

13

In Too Deep

From the time that I gave that testimony during service at Oil of Joy Ministries I began to change my life. It was the day I truly began to walk "My" walk. The day I would walk away from all I'd known for the past thirteen years of my life; how would I do that? I didn't have a clue. The only thing I could do was take it one day at a time. I took it step-by-step, one foot in front of the other.

I began my walk with Christ. There were so many different things that began to come to light. The more my teachers (my pastor and God) taught me, the more different things in my life became evident. The more I read, the more understood. I began to learn about generational curses. This spiritual growth helped me understand how we accept things in our families from previous generations. We settle for it like it's the norm. If it was poverty we accepted it, if it was lack we accepted it, if it was molestation, we accepted it, if it was addiction, we accepted it. If my grandmother drank, and my mother drank, then I drank.

But then I learned that anything did not have to go. I didn't have to settle for less, we don't have to settle for anything less. I didn't have to be poor. I don't have to deal with being a drunk. I didn't have to suffer from the shame of being molested and feeling like I did something for such a disgustingly horrible thing to happen to me. But again, even though I didn't know it, I began to seek him, more and more. The change in my life seemed to be solid. Or so I thought.

I met someone in the church and for the most part she seemed to be cool.

Snare

One day this woman was actually a little too cool because she and I actually ended up sleeping together. Let me be clear about something; I didn't do it because I cared, I did

The Colors of My Wings

it because I could and I didn't want to let go of who I thought I was. I just didn't know what that looked like and surely didn't know what it felt like. Like I told you before: I'm not one to lie. I'm not going to slip and slide and hide my actions from anyone for any reason. I'm not good at lying. I felt bad enough that I discussed it with my pastor. After that I removed that plague from my life and took another step forward.

From there, I continued to move and my faith continued to grow. My pastor would commend me and tell me I was actually doing well, especially for a "baby" in Christ. She talked to me about the quick work that the Lord was doing in me. I felt good and proud, real proud, so proud. I wanted to stay in God's good grace. I felt like He was so close to me; always watching over me. So between God and my Pastor I just wanted to do the right thing.

About four or five months into my walk, I hit a major

Snare

A childhood friend came home. I knew she was bisexual;

The Colors of My Wings

I knew she was married but separated; I knew she was going through a lot. I even knew that she was interested in me. We ended up spending time together as friends. I tried to be there when she needed me, and the need began to grow in both of us. Instead of removing myself, I allowed us to bond. I wanted to be strong enough to stay in God's will but I wasn't – not yet. We as a people have to realize that nothing is done in our strength.

A final word: Be strong in the Lord and in his mighty power,

Ephesians 6:10

If we could do it, it would already be done, and we wouldn't need God. What we must come to understand is that our will is not what He wants. God wants us to discover that we need him and through precarious circumstances we do come to realize that we can't do this alone. I did it alright; I did her and she did me. She made me feel real good too, physically that is.

However when I was done I felt horrible. I felt like I had lost a part of me; a part that I had finally found. But then it was gone again. I felt lost all over again. Here I was trying to walk this walk and BAM I screwed up, again. I had been doing so well up until this point.

Tara and I kept seeing each other. But honestly, I didn't trust her or myself, although we continued to date. Then my pastor began to ask me questions...

God

"Hey Z, are you okay?"

Of course I would say yes and try to play it off, which I'm not good at, at all. Eventually I broke down, and told her what was going on between Tara and I. I even went as far as to invite Tara to my church. As a matter of fact Tara knew the bible like the back of her hand, but it didn't matter to her, she was going to do her and appease that flesh. But it mattered to me – it mattered to me a lot. I felt hypocritical, guilty, like I let God down.

The Colors of My Wings

Here I was, falling hard; I knew I needed help. I cried, prayed and decided to go to my Pastor for prayer and direction. After talking to my pastor, she told me to restrain myself from any type of communication, especially physical contact, with Tara.

It was the night before I was instructed to begin my 21- day consecration. Tara came over to see me. We were just chilling in the bed talking about everything that had taken place between us. We began talking about her kids and the reason why she didn't have her kids.

She wound up telling me that she had a serious health issue. From what I gathered she spoke like there was a possibility of her not being here for her kids. Her attitude was why fight for them. She was basically saying maybe they were in the best place they could be, since she might not live to see them grow. That blew me away. I felt she was being selfish.

Then all of a sudden Tara began to cry so I held her and wiped her tears. She cried even harder. She suddenly jumped off the bed and ran in the bathroom and closed the door. This really bothered me. What could I do? I sat there, worried. Before I knew it, I was standing at the bathroom door asking her if she was okay. Tara didn't say anything. Not a peep. So I opened the door.

She was just sitting on the floor, crying. I sat next to her. I was right there with her; I wanted her to know that. She began to speak faintly. She took a deep breath and began to tell me why she broke down, "Zanetta: while you were holding me I felt pain in your touch."

I was like, huh, I don't get it? Tara told me that while we were lying in the bed, she had a vision of a woman's body lying on an operating table. As she walked around the table, to her surprise, the woman was her. Every time they cut her she felt pain, which was what she felt as I touched her. She continued to tell me that while she was being operated on, she also noticed all these people surrounding her, but they were not actually people, they were demons, just waiting on her to die. She cried even harder, and began to vomit.

She was spitting up over and over again. Then she told me that God spoke to her and told her that He had given her chance after chance after chance to get it right and that he was getting tired of her and her ways. Then she said, "Zanetta, close the door and go plead the blood of Jesus over your entire house."

In that moment I wanted to call my pastor, but how could I explain what Tara was doing here? But she wanted me to call Telma. I did, and they talked. Shortly afterwards she left. Now you know I wasn't going to just leave it like that. I needed some answers. I spoke to my Pastor about it and of course she tore me a new one for not being obedient. She said, "Zanetta, God must really love you. He is showing you things that a lot of people don't see so early in there Christian walk."

My Pastor also told me that the Lord really loved me and that he was fighting for my freedom.

The Colors of My Wings

147

14

The Messengers

There is always a new day when the night comes to its close. After all that, I felt like it was exactly that, a new day. I was ready to give it my all again because I loved me some Jesus. He's the one that wiped the tears away, gave me life again; gave me hope and gave me the Oil of Joy.

So the next day I got on a plane to Las Vegas to meet family members that I had never met before. I really needed to get away from Florida. I felt that would help me not to talk to Tara until I was strong enough to resist. But while I was gone, I battled with myself. I battled in my flesh about what I needed and wanted to do. I began contemplating walking away from this test and just going back to my old ways. This time I had made up my mind;

The Colors of My Wings

I could not do this any longer. I was going to give up. It was too hard to deny myself of what was natural to me – women.

While in Las Vegas my cousin and I decided to attend church. I was sitting there in this big church and again the next thing I knew, I was weeping. I sat there just listening and weeping. Then out the blue this lady that I didn't know from Adam walked up to me and hugged me. She said, "I know you are scared, but God said just trust him."

Then she went on to minister me, telling me how people thought of me as rebellious and that even my family didn't believe me. She said, but don't give up, don't let go, hold on I was like, what? I don't even know this woman. She was talking to me like she knew me. Right then I said, okay, God, I hear you. Later that day I called my Pastor. I told my Pastor what had happened at the ministry in Vegas. I told her that I was ready to give up and God spoke to me through this lady. My pastor said, "Zanetta, I already knew."

The Colors of My Wings

She also felt it in the spirit. She felt the struggle within me. So fast-forward. Now I'm back in Florida and I'm in an early morning prayer service. A young lady by the name of Shawn came to me and said, "Zanetta, God told me to tell you that he loves you, and so do I."

She told me that God told her to tell me to hold on, don't let go, and that he knows that it's hard, but to keep fighting. So again I continued to press my way, one foot in front of the other, day by day. This was the exact word I'd gotten at that ministry in Vegas.

When my pastor and I talked about what had happen before I left she told me God was really fighting for me because he allowed something so powerful to manifest itself in my life. She felt like the Lord showed me these things for a reason, then to have two different people on two different sides of the United States of America tell me the same thing; neither one of them knew what I was dealing with at the time – one of them didn't know me at all – that really let me know that my father was real and that He loved me.

So now I had to figure out how to love him the way he loved me; trust him the way he trusted me. I knew

The Colors of My Wings

somehow, some way, one day, I would get it right.

The Colors of My Wings

The Colors of My Wings

15

Recovery

My pastor had this saying, "You have to lay low." Even her husband our beloved Elder Larry Jackson who we all affectionately call "Paw Paw" would say, "You have to learn to change your people, places, and things."

These two statements helped shift my thinking, position and focus. I began spending more time alone, "laying low." I removed certain people, places and things from my life. I had already for the most part stopped drinking. Eventually, I completely stopped drinking. It's not like you would go to hell for drinking, but nothing that you do in excess aside from God's work is healthy. Once I began implementing these steps in my life, layers began to shed off me – gone.

The only voice I began to listen to was the voice of God. I read his word and listened to him. I began to make choices rather than allowing my flesh to lead me or the devil to take the wheel. I put everything in God's

The Colors of My Wings

hands and I left it there. The Lord instructed me to get rid of my cd collection. Now anyone who knows me knows that music is my first love. I had over 1,000 cds, so I was like, God, you want me to do what? At first, I didn't listen, I just gave away all of my rap music and I said, ok, God, I gave away the rap. I'm just going to put the rest under my bed, for whenever the Lord decided to bring me a husband – isn't that funny, stupid and crazy all rolled up in one?

I can't help but think about all of the blessings I lost by not being obedient and here I am trying to bargain with the Lord when I had been gambling all my life. But when I tell you that it was his goodness, mercy and grace that saved me, I mean it.

> *Then the Lord your God will restore your fortunes. He will have mercy on you and gather you back from all the nations where he has scattered you,*
>
> *Deuteronomy 30:3*

The Colors of My Wings

I had to be crazy. The one thing He (the Lord) asked me to do, I didn't do. Thinking back, all I can say is wow, how stupid of me? So one day I said to myself, okay, the next time he tells me to get rid of my music I will, no questions. But then I didn't hear from him for the longest.

Until one day I said, Zanetta, you know you're being stupid, right? He told me one time and that was enough, so I got rid of my CD's just like that and at this point I realized the battle was not mine, it was the Lord's.

And everyone assembled here will know that the Lord rescues his people, but not with sword and spear. This is the Lord's battle, and he will give you to us.

1 Samuel 17:47

From that day on I knew that I was going to be okay. I knew my son was going to be okay. At the end of the day that's all that mattered to me. Nothing that I did before, and no matter what it looked like now, could

The Colors of My Wings

make me doubt God's love for me.

I realized that I could do all things through Christ, who strengthen me, no matter how many times I fell short. All things are working together for my good and that my latter will be greater, as long as I would be obedient unto him.

I realized that because I was his daughter poverty, lack, oppression, depression, all my fears, didn't exist any more because my God is who He says He is, and I know that my daddy was going to take care of my every need.

And now that my life had gotten a little more clarification, it was like, dang, all these things that the devil had planned for me; my GOD has turned around for my greater good.

The Colors of My Wings

16

Hungry

By now it's been a year and six months since this new life, this newfound freedom, began. At this time and place I'm at another crossroad. I know the chains of bondage have been broken from me; they are no longer a strong hold on my life. So now, what? Now, I go north.

I'm looking up; keeping my eyes on the Lord. The Lord has struck a match in me and he just keeps adding fuel to the fire. Yeah, I'm on fire. I'm so hungry for life right now, yours and mine. Let me say this: Thank you for reading my testimony and for reading my story.

This book was not something I did to become an author; but I had a heart to touch others who just maybe have been through, or even still stuck, in the life as we

The Colors of My Wings

call it.

Life is interesting, according to how people figure you out. I seem to always get the same question. This particular question is not necessarily judgment but curiosity. They don't understand and simply want answers.

At times I feel bad because I always get this question. At one point in time I honestly did not know how to answer it. "Zanetta, if you are gay, how can you just change?"

I ponder for a minute. All I can say is, "Honestly, changing my life had nothing to do with Zanetta; but everything to do with God."

This was my most truthful and honest response. The only part I played in my life change was that I made myself available to Christ. That's what I tell people. Because honestly I feel like this, if Zanetta could have continued to live that life of a "lesbian", Zanetta would have. Or better yet I would have continued to allow my flesh to cry out for what it wanted when it wanted; it would have kept me bound. At the time, I felt like that's who I was and who He created me to be. I would have

The Colors of My Wings

still been living that lifestyle because I loved women.

I should say I thought it was love, because until now, I realized I really never knew what love was. So again I say, I'm hungry, I'm hungry for life and I am hungry for Christ. I will continue to allow Christ to order my steps; for me, there is no other way.

So all I can say is bread of heaven feed me until I want no more.

It is my prayer that I stay hungry for the things of God and his complete will for my life. I pray that I continue to seek his face, no matter how hard it may get because my bottom line is this: God lost his son and Jesus lost his LIFE so that my seed and I could have a chance at a better life, be it here or in heaven. That's what I'm striving for – a better life.

The Colors of My Wings

17

Challenge

For those of you who don't know Christ I challenge you. I challenge you to do nothing more than be available. Be available to receive a love like no other. I challenge you to let go and let God be the head of your life. If you can do that, watch how the Lord creates miracles, signs, and wonders in you, through you, by you.

All I know is when I allowed God to be the head, everything else fell into place. The key was that I had to completely remove Zanetta from the equation. My prayer for you is that you give Christ the opportunity to work in your life.

Now I know there will be those who are offended because they may feel I'm being a hypocrite. But the truth of the matter is this: it's my story, my journey and my

The Colors of My Wings

walk…told my way. It is never my intent to ever offend any one person or group of people, nor is it my place to judge. My heart, my life, my vision
and goals are pure. I'm just here to love all people.

So know that I love you, may the Lord continue to be a blessing as He guides you wherever He may.

So here is to new beginnings and new endings. What the devil thought he had destroyed the Lord has turned it around for my good. Please stay blessed...

Love Always,
Zanetta

The Colors of My Wings

18

Liberated

Now that I have chosen to release my past, my emotions and feelings about where I've been and how I've viewed things, I am more than ready to move forward in my new life as a new vessel in Christ Jesus. I am not allowing my past to dictate my present or my future because the enemy will try to do just that. If you give the enemy charge over your life he will keep you caught up in the things of the past.

Understand this: my history is just that, it's gone. Furthermore, it has now become "His Story" because I owe it all to Him. Concerning me: I'm prepared for "traditional Christians," or should I say, "Religious Individuals" and many others who may turn their noses up at my life story.

But I'm cool with that; they too have a process. This is my life and my story and the Lord saw fit to give me a mind, a pen, and voice to lift him up. No matter what the next man's thought process is about my book, that's fine; it's their opinion. I just pray that they will understand that I am not glorifying an act I am glorifying God and taking you through the private quarters of my testimony.

Homosexuality is an extreme strong hold. The truth of the matter is that it is a difficult reality to change everything that you once thought you were. Needless to say my sexuality was not the only issue that I battled with for many years. There were so many hurtful experiences that deeply wounded me and confused me, respective to my identity.

So I celebrate the victory that through and with Christ I walk in today.

The Lord gave me my life back therefore I'm going to be just as radical for Christ as I was when I was in the world. In summary I say this: what ever it is that you struggle with, don't feel like it's the end all be all.

Don't allow your circumstances to dictate who God ordained you to be. The enemy sends set backs to rob you of your true peace, purpose and success as a

The Colors of My Wings

Kingdom receiver.

As for me, right about now, I am unstoppable. I promise you, it's something you can be as well.

The Colors of My Wings

Closing Remarks

The Lord gave me this message:

"I knew you before I formed you in your mother's womb. Before you were born, I set you apart and appointed you as my prophet to the nations."

"O Sovereign LORD," I said, "I can't speak for you. I'm too young."

The LORD replied, "Don't say, 'I'm too young,' for you must go wherever I send you and say whatever I tell you. And don't be afraid of the people, for I will be with you and will protect you. I, the LORD, have spoken."

Then the LORD reached out and touched my mouth and said, "Look, I have put my words in your mouth. Today I appoint you to stand up against nations and kingdoms. Some you must uproot and tear down, destroy and overthrow. Others you must build up and plant."

Jeremiah 1: 4-10

The Colors of My Wings

CPSIA information can be obtained at www.ICGtesting.com
Printed in the USA
LVOW071225090213

319419LV00001B/1/P